What People Are Saying about *Threshold Bible Study*

"Abraham and Sarah are central to the biblical narrative, so it is good to see Stephen Binz drawing our attention not only to the Abrahamic narrative, but also to these ancestors in other parts of the Old and New Testaments. The focus of this well-written and accessible work is rightly on the biblical text itself, and the commentary and questions push us back to the text to listen for God's address."

■ **Craig G. Bartholomew**, *Director of the Kirby Laing Centre for Public Theology in Cambridge, England, author of* ***The Drama of Scripture***

"Using the story of Abraham and Sarah, as well as the New Testament writers' reinterpretations of elements of that story, Stephen Binz both introduces lay readers to these important biblical characters and weds serious study and personal prayer within a reflective context. He is to be applauded for this fine addition to Bible study programs."

■ **Dianne Bergant, CSA**, *Professor Emerita, Catholic Theological Union, Chicago*

"This is the perfect practice for studying the life, struggles, and hopes of Abraham and Sarah and their dynamic significance for the faith and outreach of each one of us. Stephen Binz has done a splendid job of introducing his readers to this biblical method and immersing them in it. I eagerly suggest this work—and the entire series—as the basis for your next personal or group study."

■ **Marva J. Dawn**, *Former Teaching Fellow in Spiritual Theology at Regent College in Vancouver, British Columbia*

"God's holy word addresses the deepest levels of our lives with the assurance of divine grace and wisdom for our individual and communal faith. I am grateful for *Threshold Bible Study*, helping our Catholic people explore the riches of sacred Scripture. May these guides to understanding the great truths of our Redemption bring us all closer to the Lord of our salvation."

■ **Cardinal Timothy M. Dolan**, *Archbishop of New York*

"*Threshold Bible Study* offers solid scholarship and spiritual depth. Drawing on the Church's living Tradition and the Jewish roots of the New Testament, *Threshold Bible Study* can be counted on for lively individual study and prayer, even while it offers spiritual riches to deepen communal conversation and reflection among the people of God."

■ **Scott Hahn**, *Professor of Biblical Theology, Franciscan University of Steubenville*

"*Threshold Bible Study* is a refreshing approach to enable participants to ponder the Scriptures more deeply. The thematic material is clearly presented with a mix of information and spiritual nourishment. The questions are thoughtful and the principles for group discussion are quite helpful. This series provides a practical way for faithful people to get to know the Bible better and to enjoy the fruits of biblical prayer."

Irene Nowell, OSB, *Mount St. Scholastica, Atchison, Kansas*

"*Threshold Bible Study* is appropriately named, for its commentary and study questions bring people to the threshold of the text and invite them in. The questions guide but do not dominate. They lead readers to ponder and wrestle with the biblical passages and take them across the threshold toward life with God. Stephen Binz's work stands in the tradition of the biblical renewal movement and brings it back to life. We need more of this in the Church."

Kathleen M. O'Connor, *Professor Emerita of Old Testament, Columbia Theological Seminary*

"I most strongly recommend Stephen Binz's *Threshold Bible Study* for adult Bible classes, religious education, and personal spiritual enrichment. The series is exceptional for its scholarly solidity, pastoral practicality, and clarity of presentation. The Church owes Binz a great debt of gratitude for his generous and competent labor in the service of the word of God."

Peter C. Phan, *The Ignacio Ellacuria Professor of Catholic Social Thought, Georgetown University*

"Stephen Binz has undertaken the important project of leading non-professional but committed readers of the Bible into a spiritually enlivening encounter with the biblical text through engagement with some of the fascinating characters who people its pages. This series leads the reader from Bible study to personal prayer, community involvement, and active Christian commitment in the world."

Sandra M. Schneiders, *Professor Emerita, Jesuit School of Theology at Santa Clara University*

"Stephen Binz has created an essential resource for the new evangelization rooted in the discipleship process that helps participants to unpack the treasures of the Scriptures in an engaging and accessible manner. *Threshold Bible Study* connects faith learning to faithful living leading one to a deeper relationship with Christ and his body, the Church."

Julianne Stanz, *Director of Outreach for Evangelization and Discipleship for Loyola Press*

"*Threshold Bible Study* provides a very engaging approach and encounter with sacred Scripture, all the while encouraging the faithful to listen and discern the word of God, especially in and through Jesus Christ."

Archbishop Charles C. Thompson, *Archbishop of Indianapolis*

Abraham and Sarah

Rock and Quarry of Faith

Stephen J. Binz

TWENTY-THIRD PUBLICATIONS
977 Hartford Turnpike Unit A
Waterford, CT 06385
(860) 437-3012 or (800) 321-0411
twentythirdpublications.com

ISBN: 978-1-62785-852-6
Printed in the U.S.A.

Contents

LESSONS 13–18

LESSONS 19–24

LESSONS 25–30

How to Use *Threshold Bible Study*

Threshold Bible Study is a dynamic, informative, inspiring, and life-changing series that helps you learn about Scripture in a whole new way. Each book will help you explore new dimensions of faith and discover deeper insights for your life as a disciple of Jesus.

The threshold is a place of transition. The threshold of God's word invites you to enter that place where God's truth, goodness, and beauty can shine into your life and fill your mind and heart. Through the Holy Spirit, the threshold becomes holy ground, sacred space, and graced time. God can teach you best at the threshold, because God opens your life to his word and fills you with the Spirit of truth.

With *Threshold Bible Study* each topic or book of the Bible is approached in a thematic way. You will understand and reflect on the biblical texts through overarching themes derived from biblical theology. Through this method, the study of Scripture will impact your life in a unique way and transform you from within.

These books are designed for maximum flexibility. Each study is presented in a workbook format, with sections for reading, reflecting, writing, discussing, and praying. Each *Threshold* book contains thirty lessons, which you can use for your daily study over the course of a month or which can be divided into six lessons per week, providing a group study of six weekly sessions. These studies are ideal for Bible study groups, small Christian communities, adult faith formation, student groups, Sunday school, neighborhood groups, and family reading, as well as for individual learning.

The commentary that follows each biblical passage launches your reflection on that passage and helps you begin to see its significance within the context of your contemporary experience. The questions following the commentary challenge you to understand the passage more fully and apply it to your own life. Space for writing after each question is ideal for personal study and also allows group participants to prepare in advance for the weekly discussion. The prayer helps conclude your study each day by integrating your learning into your relationship with God.

The method of *Threshold Bible Study* is rooted in the ancient tradition of *lectio divina*, whereby studying the Bible becomes a means of deeper intimacy with God and a transformed life. Reading and interpreting the text (*lectio*) is followed by reflective meditation on its message (*meditatio*). This reading and reflecting flows into prayer from the heart (*oratio* and *contemplatio*). In this way, one listens to God through the Scripture and then responds to God in prayer.

This ancient method assures you that Bible study is a matter of both the mind and the heart. It is not just an intellectual exercise to learn more and be able to discuss the Bible with others. It is, more importantly, a transforming experience. Reflecting on God's word, guided by the Holy Spirit, illumines the mind with wisdom and stirs the heart with zeal.

Following the personal Bible study, *Threshold Bible Study* offers ways to extend personal *lectio divina* into a weekly conversation with others. This communal experience will allow participants to enhance their appreciation of the message and build up a spiritual community (*collatio*). The end result will be to increase both individual faith and faithful witness in the context of daily life (*operatio*).

When bringing *Threshold Bible Study* to a church community, try to make every effort to include as many people as possible. Many will want to study on their own; others will want to study with family, a group of friends, or a few work associates; some may want to commit themselves to share insights through a weekly conference call, daily text messaging, or an online social network; and others will want to gather weekly in established small groups.

By encouraging *Threshold Bible Study* and respecting the many ways people desire to make Bible study a regular part of their lives, you will widen the number of people in your church community who study the Bible regularly in whatever way they are able in their busy lives. Simply sign up people at the Sunday services and order bulk quantities for your church. Encourage people to follow the daily study as faithfully as they can. This encouragement can be through Sunday announcements, notices in parish publications, support on the church website, and other creative invitations and motivations.

Through the spiritual disciplines of Scripture reading, study, reflection, conversation, and prayer, *Threshold Bible Study* will help you experience God's grace more abundantly and root your life more deeply in Christ. The risen Jesus said: "Listen! I am standing at the door, knocking; if you hear my voice and open the door, I will come in to you and eat with you, and you with me" (Rev 3:20). Listen to the Word of God, open the door, and cross the threshold to an unimaginable dwelling with God!

SUGGESTIONS FOR INDIVIDUAL STUDY

- Make your Bible reading a time of prayer. Ask for God's guidance as you read the Scriptures.
- Try to study daily, or as often as possible according to the circumstances of your life.
- Read the Bible passage carefully, trying to understand both its meaning and its personal application as you read. Some persons find it helpful to read the passage aloud.
- Read the passage in another Bible translation. Each version adds to your understanding of the original text.
- Allow the commentary to help you comprehend and apply the scriptural text. The commentary is only a beginning, not the last word, on the meaning of the passage.
- After reflecting on each question, write out your responses. The very act of writing will help you clarify your thoughts, bring new insights, and amplify your understanding.
- As you reflect on your answers, think about how you can live God's word in the context of your daily life.
- Conclude each daily lesson by reading the prayer and continuing with your own prayer from the heart.
- Make sure your reflections and prayers are matters of both the mind and the heart. A true encounter with God's word is always a transforming experience.
- Choose a word or a phrase from the lesson to carry with you throughout the day as a reminder of your encounter with God's life-changing word.
- For additional insights and affirmation, share your learning experience with at least one other person whom you trust. The ideal way to share learning is in a small group that meets regularly.

SUGGESTIONS FOR GROUP STUDY

- Meet regularly; weekly is ideal. Try to be on time and make attendance a high priority for the sake of the group. The average group meets for about an hour.
- Open each session with a prepared prayer, a song, or a reflection. Find some appropriate way to bring the group from the workaday world into a sacred time of graced sharing.
- If you have not been together before, name tags are very helpful as a group begins to become acquainted with the other group members.
- Spend the first session getting acquainted with one another, reading the Introduction aloud, and discussing the questions that follow.
- Appoint a group facilitator to provide guidance to the discussion. The role of facilitator may rotate among members each week. The facilitator simply keeps the discussion on track; each person shares responsibility for the group. There is no need for the facilitator to be a trained teacher.
- Try to study the six lessons on your own during the week. When you have done your own reflection and written your own answers, you will be better prepared to discuss the six scriptural lessons with the group. If you have not had an opportunity to study the passages during the week, meet with the group anyway to share support and insights.
- Participate in the discussion as much as you are able, offering your thoughts, insights, feelings, and decisions. You learn by sharing with others the fruits of your study.
- Be careful not to dominate the discussion. It is important that everyone in the group be offered an equal opportunity to share the results of their work. Try to link what you say to the comments of others so that the group remains on the topic.
- When discussing your own personal thoughts or feelings, use "I" language. Be as personal and honest as appropriate and be very cautious about giving advice to others.

- Listen attentively to the other members of the group so as to learn from their insights. The words of the Bible affect each person in a different way, so a group provides a wealth of understanding for each member.
- Don't fear silence. Silence in a group is as important as silence in personal study. It allows individuals time to listen to the voice of God's Spirit and the opportunity to form their thoughts before they speak.
- Solicit several responses for each question. The thoughts of different people will build on the answers of others and will lead to deeper insights for all.
- Don't fear controversy. Differences of opinions are a sign of a healthy and honest group. If you cannot resolve an issue, continue on, agreeing to disagree. There is probably some truth in each viewpoint.
- Discuss the questions that seem most important for the group. There is no need to cover all the questions in the group session.
- Realize that some questions about the Bible cannot be resolved, even by experts. Don't get stuck on some issue for which there are no clear answers.
- Whatever is said in the group is said in confidence and should be regarded as such.
- Pray as a group in whatever way feels comfortable. Pray for the members of your group throughout the week.

Schedule for Group Study

SESSION 1: INTRODUCTION DATE: ______________________

SESSION 2: LESSONS 1–6 DATE: ______________________

SESSION 3: LESSONS 7–12 DATE: ______________________

SESSION 4: LESSONS 13–18 DATE: ______________________

SESSION 5: LESSONS 19–24 DATE: ______________________

SESSION 6: LESSONS 25–30 DATE: ______________________

Listen to me, you that pursue righteousness, you that seek the Lord. Look to the rock from which you were hewn, and to the quarry from which you were dug. Look to Abraham your father and to Sarah who bore you. ISAIAH 51:1–2

Abraham and Sarah: Rock and Quarry of Faith

As patriarch and matriarch of the Judeo-Christian tradition, Abraham and Sarah stand at the wellspring of salvation history. The legacy of their faith has inspired God's people in every age for thousands of years. Even during times of destruction and exile, the prophets called on the example of Israel's patriarch and matriarch to offer courage and support to the struggling generations. Whenever God's people are weak and scattered, the heritage of father Abraham and mother Sarah offers a future full of hope.

Isaiah the prophet spoke the Lord's word to the people of Judah about their captivity in Babylon, urging them to pursue righteousness by looking to the rock and the quarry, the noble lives of their ancestors (Isa 51:1–2). The prophet describes Abraham as the "rock" from which his descendants were carved and Sarah as the "quarry" from which her descendants were hewn. The masculine image of rock suggests an indestructible foundation of solid faith from which later generations are shaped, while the feminine image of quarry implies a rich source from which offspring are mined. Abraham is the sturdy rock of durable stone, withstanding all the trials and tests involved in his noble vocation. Sarah is the deep pit in which are buried valuable minerals and undiscovered treasures, the abundant source from which living stones in every generation can be excavated.

As Isaiah speaks to the Jewish exiles, he is preparing them to make the same journey—from Babylon to Jerusalem—made by Abraham and Sarah over a millennia before. He is urging them to maintain hope, even when reasons to hope are hard to find. The prophet encourages the exiles to trust in God's promises like Abraham and Sarah, who waited generations for their child to be born. By summoning the faith of their ancestors, Isaiah implores the people of Judah to anticipate the future when their descendants would be numerous as the stars.

When God called Abraham and Sarah to leave their homeland and travel to a new land, the nation of Israel was composed of only one faithful couple. Then out of Abraham and Sarah came a mighty people which, during the exile, had been persecuted, slaughtered, deported, and reduced to a remnant. But God can make even greater things out of a small and faithful remnant than from a devoted couple. By looking to the loyal legacy of Abraham and the numberless offspring that came from the womb of Sarah, God's people could trust in God's faithfulness and know that the Lord would prosper their future. When God calls his people, he also blesses them. When God blesses them, their blessings multiply.

Reflection and discussion

- Why are "rock" and "quarry" such durable metaphors for Israel's patriarch and matriarch?

- Who are the people I would define as my fathers and mothers—biologically, ethnically, and spiritually?

The Unity of Abraham and Sarah

Although the Bible doesn't give us too many particulars about the daily relationship of the father and mother of Israel, the challenges of their lives demonstrate that they shared a great deal of love for each other. They moved together when God told them to move, even though they were not sure where they were going. They faced a famine together, probably more than once. And perhaps the most trying experience for both of them was their infertility for many, many years. Even the poor decision of Abram to have a son with Sarai's servant, Hagar, was done for the sake of their marriage and their future together.

By the time God changed the names of Abram and Sarai to Abraham and Sarah, they had lived a lifetime of faith-testing circumstances. The Scriptures don't idealize Israel's ancestors; it portrays Abraham and Sarah as real people, with conflicting emotions and fallible understanding. Abraham courageously followed God's call, yet his fear of the pharaoh and King Abimelech induced him to lie about the status of his wife, identifying her as his sister, a heartbreaking experience for Sarah. Willing to arrange for her servant Hagar to bear her husband a child, Sarah later out of jealousy ordered Abraham to cast them out. Although Sarah willingly joined her husband's religious quest, she laughed in disbelief when she received her own revelation about the forthcoming birth of a son.

After Sarah's death, Abraham mourned for her and purchased a field that would contain her burial place. This was the only land Abraham ever owned in Canaan. He purchased the field not only to bury Sarah but to express his confidence in God's promises. He had lived for sixty years as a nomad in the land, but before he himself died, he mingled the dust of his love with that of the promised land as a sign of his expectation that God would fulfill the promises for his descendants.

So, we have much to learn from studying our first couple. Their story is one full of sorrows and troubles and at the same time great joy and triumph. They worked together as spouses and as partners in a holy alliance with God. Their story is important to us not because of their perfect choices or faithfulness, but because they experienced real doubts and struggles even amid God's plans and promises. From them we see the pain that comes from disobedience to God, and we learn that trusting God is the only way to live.

Abraham and Sarah did not deny the difficult circumstances of their lives, but they looked beyond them. While acknowledging their struggles, accepting the facts of old age and barrenness, they did not weaken in faith. As children of Abraham and Sarah, we too must walk as people of hope. Dealing honestly with our circumstances, we must look beyond them to the truth of what Scripture reveals about God, his guidance, and his ability to fulfill his word.

While Abraham and Sarah waited in hope, they continued to give praise and worship to God. Instead of focusing on their own difficult circumstances, they thanked God for his goodness. Living in this way enabled them to experience God working on their behalf many times through the years, and they knew that God had the power to do what he had promised, no matter how impossible it appeared. We too must live in confident prayer, looking to God and giving glory to him. Such worship of God empowers us to continue hoping against hope.

Although Abraham and Sarah stumbled often, sinning against God and doubting the divine plan, in God's account they are described as people who did not waver, who walked in trusting faith. So, when we are struggling with hope or battling unbelief, we can know that God keeps account very differently than we do. God views us through the lens of grace. When we repent, God's grace more than covers our weakness.

Through it all, Abraham and Sarah were faithful to each other and, ultimately, faithful to the Lord. What joy filled their heart when they finally cradled their infant son Isaac, rejoicing at God's power displayed through their weakness. His birth shouts with confidence that God fulfills his promises. Their story challenges us to view our lives from God's perspective. As sons and daughters of Abraham and Sarah, we too can step into the unknown, trusting God to deliver on his promises. So from this one couple, who were as good as dead, came descendants "as many as the stars of heaven and as the innumerable grains of sand by the seashore" (Hebrews 11:12).

Reflection and discussion

- What stands out most about Abraham and Sarah's relationship?

- What do I want to learn from these spiritual parents for my own life?

Divine Names and Sacred Places

The biblical account of Abraham and Sarah begins in Mesopotamia, where their families served other gods. But as God leads them to Canaan, they come to experience God in many places and circumstances as they pass through the promised land. As we study these accounts, we will discover a variety of names for God and see the impact of God's ongoing revelation. At each stage of travel, first at Shechem and then near Bethel, Abraham pitched his tent, "built an altar to the Lord and invoked the name of the Lord" (Gen 12:6–8).

During Abram's meeting with Melchizedek at the gates of Salem, the priest-king introduced the patriarch to another of God's names: El Elyon, translated as "God Most High." The name speaks of God's sovereignty, his elevated status above all of creation. Melchizedek gave his blessing to Abram saying, "Blessed by Abram by God Most High, maker of heaven and earth" (Gen 14:19). Abram was learning that he could depend upon the might of God to protect his family from harm.

The next divine name is revealed through the experiences of Hagar, the servant of Abram and Sarai. After the pregnant Hagar is cast out of their home because of Sarai's harsh treatment of her, God sees the servant in the wilderness and calls her by name, promising to make her the mother of a great people. Hagar gives God the name El-roi, the God whom I have seen, the God who sees me (Gen 16:13). She realizes that El-roi saw her in her distress, and she testifies that God is a God who sees all. When she has no one else and nowhere to turn, God was there to reassure her. Single, pregnant, and no place to go, God has seen it all and comes to her help.

As God confirms the covenant with Abram, God reveals himself as El Shaddai, translated as "God Almighty" (Gen 17:1). God changes the name of Abram to Abraham, making him "the ancestor of a multitude of nations, and promises to be God to Abraham and his offspring (Gen 17:5–7). Through his son Ishmael and his future son Isaac, Abraham will be the father of two great peoples and an increasingly large segment of humanity will look upon him as its spiritual ancestor. Shaddai is rooted in the word for breast or mountain; El Shaddai means that God is all-powerful and all-sufficient. He is more than enough to sustain and bless his people as they walk before him.

As Abraham grew in prosperity, Abimelech traveled to Beer-sheba to enter into a mutual nonaggression treaty in order to protect his family, flocks, and access to the wells in the desert. Wanting to protect his children and descendants through the generations, Abimelech asked Abraham to swear an oral oath, solemnized by divine witness and the sacrifice of seven ewe lambs. To commemorate the treaty, Abraham planted a tamarisk, a slow-growing tree with deep roots, while he "called there on the name of the Everlasting God" (Gen 21:33). This divine name, El Olam, declares that God is eternal and unchanging. The name speaks to the unbreakable and unconditional covenant God had made with Abraham and his descendant.

After Abraham demonstrated his willingness to sacrifice his son Isaac, God spared the boy and provided a ram for the offering instead. Abraham then named the place after the divine name Yahweh Yireh, meaning "The Lord Will Provide." The text notes that "it is said to this day, 'On the mount of the Lord it shall be provided'" (Gen 22:14). The Lord is the one who provided the ram to be sacrificed in place of Isaac and who will continue to provide the offering for his people. As Abraham and Isaac started up one side of the mountain, God was sending a ram up the other side. God "looks ahead" (pro-vision) for us. We can always trust God to provide the sacrifice we need.

God reveals his many names at specific places and moments in redemptive history. The names of God tell us about God's character and how God chooses to unveil his attributes through the texts of Scripture. Yet, the God who revealed himself to Abraham and Sarah can never be fully known. What we know of God from the Bible is only a glimpse of the profound depths and majesty of God. The One who called Abraham to leave his homeland and wander about the land of Canaan in tents is a God who refuses to be stationary or restrained. The tradition of our patriarch and matriarch teaches that it is utterly impossible to define God fully or to confine God completely in any image, temple, or institution made from human hands.

Reflection and discussion

- Why are there so many names for the one God in the Bible and religious literature? Why has God only gradually revealed his identity and true nature to the peoples of the earth?

- What are the ways in which people through the ages have attempted to define or confine God? Why is this ultimately impossible?

The Father of All Who Believe

From the temple mount of Jerusalem, the sounds of the three great religions can be heard in the distance: the blowing of the shofar, the ringing of church bells, and the Muslim prayers amplified from the minarets. People today take for granted this dissonance of sounds. For many people of the world, these are the sounds that represent a bitter history of antagonism and conflicting worldviews. But if we look to Abraham, and if we look to the truest teachings of the founders who followed him—Moses, Jesus, and Muhammad—these three sounds could become a harmonious triad for all the world to hear the sounds of peace.

Over half of all the people on earth today look to one man as the pioneer of their relationship with God. Judaism, Christianity, and Islam trace the foundation of their belief to the encounter of Abraham with God almost four millennia ago. From him and his descendants God wishes to bring only blessings to all the families of the earth.

Abraham is truly the father of the world's monotheists. For most Jews and many Arab Christians and Muslims, that fatherhood is rooted in their DNA. But for most of the world's believers, Abraham's fatherhood has nothing at all to do with blood. All of these religions define "father" more expansively as the one who gives his children a spiritual outlook, the one who hands on to his children what he has discovered about God. The one who teaches the essential truths of life, the one who transmits tradition and identity to the next generation, is father to his spiritual descendants. For the same reason that spiritual directors, priests, and rabbis are called father by those they teach and guide, Abraham is father to us all.

The Jewish people trace their lineage back to Abraham. If their exodus from Egypt was the birth canal through which they passed to their freedom and their encounter with God on Mount Sinai the moment of birth, their conception was the covenant God made with Abraham. When God passed through the separated parts of Abraham's sacrifice with his fiery torch (Gen 15), he conceived a new people who would develop through the stages of gestation for four hundred years, through Isaac, Jacob, and their children, down to the call of Moses. All Jews look to Abraham as both the biological and spiritual beginning of their life as a people. They trace their lineage through Abraham's son Isaac, his son Jacob, and Jacob's twelve sons who were the founders of Israel's twelve tribes.

The gospels of the New Testament underscore that Jesus is a son of Abraham. Tracing his lineage through King David and back to Abraham, the evangelists accentuate the Judaism of Jesus and his messianic roots. As Israel's Messiah, Jesus brought the history of Abraham's descendants to a peak. Yet his saving mission was not limited in scope to only the children of Israel. The universal dimension of God's plan begun in Abraham, a plan to bring blessings to all the nations, began to be realized in Jesus and was spread through the evangelizing mission of his disciples. For the world's Christians, Abraham is their spiritual father, the one in whom God's history of salvation began. By belonging to Christ, Christians see themselves as Abraham's offspring, a multitude as uncountable as the stars of the sky.

In the Qu'ran of Islam, Abraham (Ibrahim, in Arabic) is the primary example of what it means to be a muslim, which means "one who submits to God." He is viewed as the true founder of Islam, and Muslims invoke him daily in prayer. The accounts of Abraham's offspring begin with a conflict between two women, one from Mesopotamia, his beloved wife Sarah; the other from Egypt, Sarah's servant Hagar. Abraham's first child, Ishmael, is born from Hagar; later Isaac is born from Sarah. The biblical stories of the two sons are strikingly balanced. Though Ishmael is expelled from Abraham's house at the insistence of Sarah, he is not excluded from Abraham's affection and paternity. Though Isaac receives the inheritance of Abraham, Ishmael is also abundantly blessed by God. There is no victor and loser here. Ishmael later marries an Egyptian and fathers twelve tribes and becomes the leader of a great nation. According to both Jewish and Islamic tradition, this great nation descended from Ishmael is the Arab people.

The Bible and the most essential traditions of Judaism, Christianity, and Islam demonstrate that the God of Abraham is not the possession of any single race or people. He lived before the historical expressions of each of these religions, and is looked upon by all as their founding ancestor. Today the truth that Abraham discovered about God is dispersed to every corner of the world. When the descendants of Abraham look back to their origin, they discover that they are all offspring of the same father, members of the same family. The carefully balanced message of the stories of Abraham is that God cares for all of his children.

Too often religion has become a font of hatred and conflict. But, in fact, the core teachings of the world's religions condemn the kinds of divisions we witness today. A growing number of people today believe that religion, when divorced from its perversion in fundamentalism, can be a source of healing and reconciliation in our world. Indeed, the great religions aspire to the highest expression of justice, healing, and harmony—the shalom of Yahweh, the saalam of Allah. Perhaps the font of lasting peace can be found at the common source of our faith in the one God. Can Abraham, long dead but certainly not forgotten, be an agent of peace in our conflicted world? What if we could truly realize what the ancient Scriptures proclaim about Abraham: "Through him, all the nations of the earth shall be blessed"?

Reflection and discussion

- In what way is Abraham the founding father of each of the three major monotheistic religions?

- In what way is the crisis in the Middle East a sibling rivalry? What could end the fighting and begin the reconciliation?

Prayer

God of Abraham, Sarah, and Hagar, you have promised blessings to all the peoples of the earth. Open my heart to a spirit of forgiveness toward those who share my life, and help me be a minister of reconciliation to struggling and broken people. May the peace you desire for the world begin through an understanding of the sacred texts of our ancestors in faith. Enlighten and encourage me as I read and contemplate your inspired word in these sacred Scriptures. Show me how to make my life a testimony to God's love.

SUGGESTIONS FOR FACILITATORS, GROUP SESSION 1

1. If the group is meeting for the first time, or if there are newcomers joining the group, it is helpful to provide nametags.

2. Distribute the books to the members of the group.

3. You may want to ask the participants to introduce themselves and tell the group a bit about themselves.

4. Ask one or more of these introductory questions:
    - What drew you to join this group?
    - What is your biggest fear in beginning this Bible study?
    - How is beginning this study like a "threshold" for you?

5. You may want to pray this prayer as a group:
   Come upon us, Holy Spirit, to enlighten and guide us as we begin this study of Abraham and Sarah. You inspired the writers of the Scriptures to reveal your presence throughout the history of salvation. This inspired word has the power to convert our hearts and change our lives. Fill our hearts with desire, trust, and confidence as you shine the light of your truth within us. Motivate us to read the Scriptures and give us a deeper love for God's word each day. Bless us during this session and throughout the coming week with the fire of your love.

6. Read the Introduction aloud, pausing at each question for discussion. Group members may wish to write down the insights of the group as each question is discussed. Encourage several members of the group to respond to each question.

7. Don't feel compelled to finish the complete Introduction during the session. It is better to allow sufficient time to talk about the questions raised than to rush to the end. Group members may read any remaining sections on their own after the group meeting.

8. Instruct group members to read the first six lessons on their own during the six days before the next group meeting. They should write out their own answers to the questions as preparation for next week's group discussion.

9. Fill in the date for each group meeting under "Schedule for Group Study."

10. Conclude by praying aloud together the prayer at the end of the Introduction.

"Go from your country and your kindred and your father's house to the land that I will show you. I will make of you a great nation, and I will bless you, and make your name great, so that you will be a blessing." GENESIS 12:1–2

Abram and Sarai Go Forth at the Call of God

GENESIS 12:1–9 1*Now the Lord said to Abram, "Go from your country and your*
kindred and your father's house to the land that I will show you. 2*I will make of you*
a great nation, and I will bless you, and make your name great, so that you will be
a blessing. 3*I will bless those who bless you, and the one who curses you I will curse;*
and in you all the families of the earth shall be blessed."

4*So Abram went, as the Lord had told him; and Lot went with him. Abram was*
seventy-five years old when he departed from Haran. 5*Abram took his wife Sarai*
and his brother's son Lot, and all the possessions that they had gathered, and the
persons whom they had acquired in Haran; and they set forth to go to the land of
Canaan. When they had come to the land of Canaan, 6*Abram passed through the*
land to the place at Shechem, to the oak of Moreh. At that time the Canaanites
were in the land. 7*Then the Lord appeared to Abram, and said, "To your offspring*
I will give this land." So he built there an altar to the Lord, who had appeared to
him. 8*From there he moved on to the hill country on the east of Bethel, and pitched*
his tent, with Bethel on the west and Ai on the east; and there he built an altar to
the Lord and invoked the name of the Lord. 9*And Abram journeyed on by stages*
toward the Negeb.

Abram had already lived much of his life. He no longer possessed the vigor of youth or the gullibility and hearty desire for fortune and fame that often characterizes young adulthood. He had earned a secure life in his Mesopotamian culture. But in the middle of life, after his father had died, Abram received the call to begin again.

God's words to Abram, "Go forth" (verse 1), present an imperative and an invitation. The enormity of what God asks and of the decision to be made is expressed through the threefold listing of what Abram must leave: "your country and your kindred and your father's house." The terms are arranged in ascending order according to the severity of the sacrifice involved: the region of Mesopotamia, his ethnic group, and his extended family. God's call demanded that he leave the basis of his security, trade, and identity. He must transfer his orientation from his homeland and his lineage to God and God's promises.

At the center of Abram's call are the wondrous promises of God. These promises are the key to the entire Bible and will be fulfilled throughout the history of salvation. The initial set of promises express God's commitment to Abram: first, to make of him a great nation; second, to bless him with abundant flocks and numerous offspring, good health and long life; and third, to make his name great so that he will be esteemed with a noble reputation (verse 2). The second set of promises show how God will affect other nations through Abram and how God will protect Abram among the nations (verse 3). Most amazingly, God proclaims the highest goal of Abram's calling: "In you all the families of the earth shall be blessed." Through Abraham and his descendants, God will bestow universal blessings to all the people of the earth.

In unwavering obedience to the divine call, Abram accepts his new identity: "Abram went" (verse 4). At age seventy-five, Abram has the vision to see beyond his own lifetime and the wisdom to understand the importance of making sacrifices for future generations. Every aging person wants to leave a legacy, and Abram's legacy would extend farther than anyone could imagine.

The journey of Abram from the homeland of his ancestors, Ur, to Haran, and then, at the call of God, to Shechem in the land of Canaan, took him along some of the most ancient roads and through some of the most important cities and lands of the ancient world. Archaeology has revealed that Shechem (verse 6) and Bethel (verse 8) were already Canaanite religious shrines before Abram arrived. Abram built altars there and worshipped God. Here God gave

Abram another promise: "To your offspring I will give this land" (verse 7). Hereafter, the history of Abram's descendant is inextricably bound to the promised land. Continuing southward, he reached the Negeb, having traversed the entire length of the land, marking out the land of promise.

Abram was a spiritual pioneer. He took the necessary risk and made the inevitable sacrifices for a future that he would never see. His every action, then, gained a significance that transcended his own lifetime and would eventually change the whole world.

Reflection and discussion

- When have I overcome the fear of change in order to make a new beginning?

- What is the legacy I want to leave beyond my own lifetime?

- In what way is Abraham a model for me of trust in the future? What can I do to demonstrate a greater trust in the future God has in store for me?

Prayer

Lord God, you called Abraham to leave his familiar homeland in order to begin again. Help me trust in your promises to me and overcome the fear of change. Give me the grace to make a fresh start and the wisdom to hope in the future.

When Abram entered Egypt the Egyptians saw that the woman was very beautiful. When the officials of Pharaoh saw her, they praised her to Pharaoh. And the woman was taken into Pharaoh's house.

GENESIS 12:14–15

Abram and Sarai in Egypt

GENESIS 12:10–20 10*Now there was a famine in the land. So Abram went down*
to Egypt to reside there as an alien, for the famine was severe in the land. 11*When*
he was about to enter Egypt, he said to his wife Sarai, "I know well that you are
a woman beautiful in appearance; 12*and when the Egyptians see you, they will*
say, 'This is his wife'; then they will kill me, but they will let you live. 13*Say you are*
my sister, so that it may go well with me because of you, and that my life may be
spared on your account." 14*When Abram entered Egypt the Egyptians saw that the*
woman was very beautiful. 15*When the officials of Pharaoh saw her, they praised*
her to Pharaoh. And the woman was taken into Pharaoh's house. 16*And for her*
sake he dealt well with Abram; and he had sheep, oxen, male donkeys, male and
female slaves, female donkeys, and camels.

17*But the Lord afflicted Pharaoh and his house with great plagues because of*
Sarai, Abram's wife. 18*So Pharaoh called Abram, and said, "What is this you have*
done to me? Why did you not tell me that she was your wife? 19*Why did you say,*
'She is my sister,' so that I took her for my wife? Now then, here is your wife, take
her, and be gone." 20*And Pharaoh gave his men orders concerning him; and they*
set him on the way, with his wife and all that he had.

The Bible consistently shows the heroes of faith as they really are, not as we might idealistically wish them to be. This account of Abram stands in sharp contrast to the trusting faith demonstrated by his response to God's call. Here the patriarch is shown in all of his human frailty, threatened by famine and physical peril, and seeking desperate solutions. When people are put in extreme circumstances, they often face excruciating choices about how to survive.

The "famine in the land" (verse 10) indicates that living in the promised land was harsh and often precarious. Though famine could result from any number of natural or human causes, the most common cause in Canaan was the failure of the seasonal rains. In contrast to Canaan, Egypt could depend on the more predictable rise of the Nile River for its rich fertility. So Abram and his wife Sarai went to live in Egypt in order to survive the famine.

Because of Sarai's surpassing beauty, Abram feared that some Egyptian might murder him in order to take her. So, Abram asked Sarai to pass herself off as his sister, which she agreed to do (verses 11–13). Jewish and Christian commentaries on this story judge Abram's conduct in a variety of ways. Some condemn Abram's choice for placing his virtuous wife in a compromising situation because of his own fear of being killed. Others describe his dilemma as a choice between two evils. If Abram told the truth, he would surely be killed and Sarai would be condemned to abuse and shame. His deception at least assured the survival of both of them.

Another judgment on this account is based on the ancient norm that, in the absence of a father, the brother assumed legal guardianship of his sister with responsibilities for arranging her marriage. Perhaps Abram reasoned that, by posing as Sarai's brother, he could force whoever wanted to take Sarai as a wife to negotiate with him. This would buy some time until the famine lifted, allowing both of them to escape and return to Canaan.

As expected, Sarai's extraordinary beauty attracted the attention of Pharaoh's officials and she was brought into the harem of Pharaoh. In turn, the Pharaoh bestowed abundant gifts on Abram in return for Sarai (verses 15–16). The helpless couple is faced with the overwhelming power of imperial Egypt. Abram is saved, but Sarai is trapped in a seemingly hopeless situation that threatens the promises God has made.

In the end, God intervenes to rescue those he has chosen (verse 17). The nature of the plague is not described, but the literature of Jewish midrash delights in describing the severe genital inflammation that must have afflicted Pharaoh as his passion for Sarai was stirred. Pharaoh is infuriated at Abram for his trickery and orders his men to escort Abram and Sarai with all their possessions out of the country (verses 18–20).

Many ancient epics recount a story of the abduction of the hero's beautiful wife. In most of these, a military campaign (even to the scope of the Trojan War) is launched to recover her. But in the epic of Abraham, God is the deliverer. The story shows the length to which God will go, when all human resources have failed, to deliver his chosen ones and to protect the promises he has made to them.

The experiences of Abram and Sarai prefigure the experience of their offspring many generations later in the Exodus. Like their ancestors, the descendants of Abram and Sarai would journey to Egypt to escape a famine in Canaan. Later, their welcome would fade and Pharaoh would subject them to his own will. In order to rescue the descendants of Abram and Sarai from bondage, God would inflict plagues upon Pharaoh, convincing Pharaoh to eject the Israelites. Escaping from Egypt ahead of Pharaoh's army, Israel would take with them all the goods they had received from the Egyptians.

Reflection and discussion

- Which of the explanations offered seems the most probable reason for Abram's desire to pass off Sarai as his sister?

- Why do the biblical authors choose to highlight the human weaknesses and shortcomings of biblical heroes? How is this helpful to me in seeking to learn from their experiences with God?

- When have I made a difficult choice in an extreme circumstance? In what way did God deliver me or come to my rescue?

- Does Abram's trick indicate a lack of trust in God? In what way is trust an essential ingredient of marriage or friendship?

Prayer

God of love, through enduring sacrifices and sharing goals, Abraham and Sarah became models of devotion. Help me to trust in you in the midst of life's adversities, and help me to imitate the dedication of my ancestors.

LESSON 3  SESSION 2

Then Abram said to Lot, "Let there be no strife between you and me, and between your herders and my herders; for we are kindred." GENESIS 13:8

The Families of Abram and Lot Separate

GENESIS 13:1–18 *1So Abram went up from Egypt, he and his wife, and all that
he had, and Lot with him, into the Negeb. 2Now Abram was very rich in livestock,
in silver, and in gold. 3He journeyed on by stages from the Negeb as far as Bethel, to
the place where his tent had been at the beginning, between Bethel and Ai, 4to the
place where he had made an altar at the first; and there Abram called on the name
of the Lord. 5Now Lot, who went with Abram, also had flocks and herds and tents,
6so that the land could not support both of them living together; for their possessions were so great that they could not live together, 7and there was strife between
the herders of Abram's livestock and the herders of Lot's livestock. At that time the
Canaanites and the Perizzites lived in the land.*

*8Then Abram said to Lot, "Let there be no strife between you and me, and
between your herders and my herders; for we are kindred. 9Is not the whole land
before you? Separate yourself from me. If you take the left hand, then I will go to
the right; or if you take the right hand, then I will go to the left." 10Lot looked about
him, and saw that the plain of the Jordan was well watered everywhere like the
garden of the Lord, like the land of Egypt, in the direction of Zoar; this was before
the Lord had destroyed Sodom and Gomorrah. 11So Lot chose for himself all the
plain of the Jordan, and Lot journeyed eastward; thus they separated from each
other. 12Abram settled in the land of Canaan, while Lot settled among the cities of*

the Plain and moved his tent as far as Sodom. [13]*Now the people of Sodom were wicked, great sinners against the Lord.*

[14]*The Lord said to Abram, after Lot had separated from him, "Raise your eyes now, and look from the place where you are, northward and southward and eastward and westward;* [15]*for all the land that you see I will give to you and to your offspring forever.* [16]*I will make your offspring like the dust of the earth; so that if one can count the dust of the earth, your offspring also can be counted.* [17]*Rise up, walk through the length and the breadth of the land, for I will give it to you."* [18]*So Abram moved his tent, and came and settled by the oaks of Mamre, which are at Hebron; and there he built an altar to the Lord.*

Lot, the nephew of Abram, had journeyed with Abram and Sarai from Haran, and now has traveled with the couple from Egypt back into the promised land (verse 1). It was customary that the oldest uncle should assume the guardianship of the child of his deceased brother. The childless Abram must have grown to love his nephew Lot as if he were his own son. Yet, there comes a time when adults must separate from their grown children and surrender them to the world outside their family. Though Abram and Sarai had deeply invested their time and love in Lot, it was now time to let go and let Lot find his own way.

In a nomadic culture in which herders were dependent on available grazing land and watering places, environmental realities placed a limit on the size of herds and encampments. With increasing friction growing between the herders of Abram's livestock and those of Lot over available pasturage and water, Abram decides to take action (verses 5–7). Showing nobility of character, Abram selflessly offers his nephew first choice of grazing land. Though one would expect Lot to defer to his uncle, Lot quickly chooses the more attractive land of the Jordan Plain (verses 8–11).

Lot's greed eventually turns out to be his downfall. Dazzled by the appearance of abundance, Lot imagined prosperity in the fertile valley and is attracted to the stimuli of the cities of the Plain (verses 12–13). Abram, on the other hand, inherits the more rugged hills of Canaan, an area where dependence on God seems more necessary, a place where trust and peace can be cultivated.

After Lot has departed, God firmly links Abram's future to the land. At God's invitation, Abram looks north toward Shechem, south toward Hebron, east toward the Jordan River, and west toward the Mediterranean. God assured Abram that this would be the land of his offspring forever (verses 14–15). His descendants, God said, will be like the dust of the earth—beyond numbering (verse 16). Finally, Abram is told to walk the length and breadth of the land (verse 17), a symbolic action indicating that the land will belong to Abram and he will belong to the land. He settled near the trees of Mamre, in the vicinity of Hebron. These great oaks served as a landmark as well as welcome shade in the hot and windy climate.

Reflection and discussion

- How did Abram know it was time to separate from Lot? How do parents and adult children know when it is time to let go and separate from one another?

- In what ways does God link Abraham's future to the land? Why is God's promise of land so important for Abraham?

- What is the land God has given me? To what places is my identity particularly bound? How does the locale in which I live help me cultivate a life for God?

Prayer

Lord God, when I look to the north, south, east, and west, I realize that I am surrounded by reminders of your presence. I want to cultivate a life that gives honor to you. Help me to treasure your gifts that surround me and to use them for your greater glory.

King Melchizedek of Salem brought out bread and wine; he was priest of God Most High. He blessed him and said, "Blessed be Abram by God Most High, maker of heaven and earth."

GENESIS 14:18–19

Abram Blessed by Melchizedek

GENESIS 14:17–24 [17]*After his [Abraham's] return from the defeat of Chedorlaomer and the kings who were with him, the king of Sodom went out to meet him at the Valley of Shaveh (that is, the King's Valley).* [18]*And King Melchizedek of Salem brought out bread and wine; he was priest of God Most High.* [19]*He blessed him and said,*

"Blessed be Abram by God Most High,
maker of heaven and earth;
[20]*and blessed be God Most High,*
who has delivered your enemies into your hand!"

And Abram gave him one tenth of everything. [21]*Then the king of Sodom said to Abram, "Give me the persons, but take the goods for yourself."* [22]*But Abram said to the king of Sodom, "I have sworn to the Lord, God Most High, maker of heaven and earth,* [23]*that I would not take a thread or a sandal-thong or anything that is yours, so that you might not say, 'I have made Abram rich.'* [24]*I will take nothing but what the young men have eaten, and the share of the men who went with me—Aner, Eshcol, and Mamre. Let them take their share."*

Genesis 14 describes a surprising new feature of Abram's personality: the courageous warrior-chieftain. A confederacy of four kings from the East had subjugated the city states of the area around the Dead Sea for many years and had returned to suppress a rebellion. While plundering Sodom and surrounding cities, the kings' forces took large amounts of booty and some captives, including Abram's nephew Lot (verses 1–12).

On learning the news of Lot's capture, Abram again demonstrates his self-sacrificing loyalty to his family in time of need. Abram mustered a force of 318 men and mounted an armed campaign to rescue his nephew. Taking advantage of darkness and surprising his foes, Abram routed the enemies. They fled so quickly that they left all the spoils, along with Lot and other captives (verses 13–16).

As Abram was returning home triumphantly, he was met by two monarchs: the king of Sodom and the king of Salem. The kings came out from their cities to meet the patriarch, whose victory had benefited the entire region. The contrast between these two kings could not be greater. The king of Sodom, whose name is not mentioned, came out to meet his benefactor empty-handed, and the first word that he uttered was "Give." The king of Salem, whose name is Melchizedek, brought out bread and wine for a victory feast with Abram and his men, and he offered a blessing for Abram.

Melchizedek is both a king and a priest, and as such he invoked a blessing on Abram (verses 18–19). Hebrew tradition identified Salem with Jerusalem (Ps 76:2), and the place where the king and patriarch met, the King's Valley (verse 17), is right outside the walls of Jerusalem. The divine name and title evoked by Melchizedek, "God Most High, maker of heaven and earth," is also the name by which Abram called upon God (verses 19–20, 22). The writer of Genesis is making the bold claim that the one God who called Abram was indistinctly known in the chief god of the Canaanite pantheon. Truly the God of Abram is the universal God who will bless all peoples of the earth. In denying any claim to the spoils he had won in war, Abram shows that his trust in God was complete (verses 22–23). He would depend on no earthly king for his wealth, but in the maker of heaven and earth.

Melchizedek is mentioned only one other time in the Hebrew Scriptures. In a royal psalm extolling the Davidic ruler of Jerusalem, it is said of the king, "You are a priest forever according to the order of Melchizedek" (Ps 110:4).

Like Melchizedek, the Canaanite predecessor of the Davidic king in the pre-Israelite Jerusalem, the Israelite king was both priest and king, chief mediator between God and people. Melchizedek's service as priest to Abram immortalized him as the model of sacred kingship and of a priestly messiah. The writer of the book of Hebrews interprets the ministry of Jesus as the fulfillment of Melchizedek's line (see Hebrews 7:1–22).

Reflection and discussion

- Abram was loyal to his nephew despite Lot's less-than-honorable treatment of his uncle. How do I respond when a member of my family is in trouble? What does the example of Abram teach me about family loyalty?

- In what way did Abram's acknowledgment of God as "maker of heaven and earth" enable him to trust? How does my understanding of God help me to trust?

- How does my understanding that Israel's Messiah is both king and priest help me to know Jesus Christ? How do I honor him as king and priest?

Prayer

Most High God, you are the creator of heaven and earth. Bind my family to you and help me to be loyal to the people you have given to me as my family. Show me how to live in trusting confidence in you and to know that you provide all that I need.

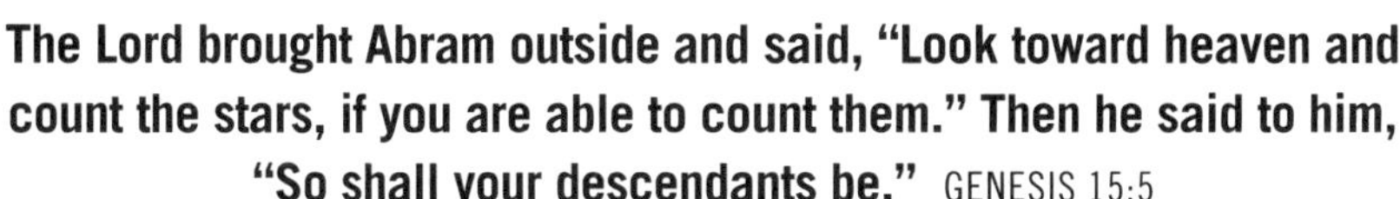

The Lord brought Abram outside and said, "Look toward heaven and count the stars, if you are able to count them." Then he said to him, "So shall your descendants be." GENESIS 15:5

God Seals the Covenant with Abram

GENESIS 15:1–21 1*After these things the word of the Lord came to Abram in*
a vision, "Do not be afraid, Abram, I am your shield; your reward shall be very
great." 2*But Abram said, "O Lord God, what will you give me, for I continue child-*
less, and the heir of my house is Eliezer of Damascus?" 3*And Abram said, "You*
have given me no offspring, and so a slave born in my house is to be my heir." 4*But*
the word of the Lord came to him, "This man shall not be your heir; no one but
your very own issue shall be your heir." 5*He brought him outside and said, "Look*
toward heaven and count the stars, if you are able to count them." Then he said to
him, "So shall your descendants be." 6*And he believed the Lord; and the Lord reck-*
oned it to him as righteousness.

7*Then he said to him, "I am the Lord who brought you from Ur of the*
Chaldeans, to give you this land to possess." 8*But he said, "O Lord God, how am*
I to know that I shall possess it?" 9*He said to him, "Bring me a heifer three years*
old, a female goat three years old, a ram three years old, a turtledove, and a young
pigeon." 10*He brought him all these and cut them in two, laying each half over*
against the other; but he did not cut the birds in two. 11*And when birds of prey*
came down on the carcasses, Abram drove them away.

12*As the sun was going down, a deep sleep fell upon Abram, and a deep and*
terrifying darkness descended upon him. 13*Then the Lord said to Abram, "Know*

this for certain, that your offspring shall be aliens in a land that is not theirs, and shall be slaves there, and they shall be oppressed for four hundred years; [14]*but I will bring judgment on the nation that they serve, and afterward they shall come out with great possessions.* [15]*As for yourself, you shall go to your ancestors in peace; you shall be buried in a good old age.* [16]*And they shall come back here in the fourth generation; for the iniquity of the Amorites is not yet complete."*

[17]*When the sun had gone down and it was dark, a smoking fire pot and a flaming torch passed between these pieces.* [18]*On that day the Lord made a covenant with Abram, saying, "To your descendants I give this land, from the river of Egypt to the great river, the river Euphrates,* [19]*the land of the Kenites, the Kenizzites, the Kadmonites,* [20]*the Hittites, the Perizzites, the Rephaim,* [21]*the Amorites, the Canaanites, the Girgashites, and the Jebusites."*

"Do not be afraid" (verse 1), God called to Abram. Faith like that of Abram does not happen in an instant. It must grow stronger over time as fears are faced and overcome. God wants Abram to believe the promise despite the logical improbabilities of its being fulfilled. The years had been passing by and the promised heir had not materialized. Again God assures Abram with another intangible promise: "Your reward shall be very great." But Abram's pent-up frustrations had reached their limit. He bursts forth with his doubts and disappointments: "O Lord God, what will you give me, for I continue childless?" (verse 2). No material reward could ever equal the blessing of having a child.

The covenant promises are divided into two sections: verses 1–5 focus on the promise of posterity; verses 7–21 focus on the gift of land. The first promise is made at night in a vision (verses 1, 5); the second takes place at sundown in a "deep sleep" (verse 12). The twin promises are interconnected; one is necessary for the other. God's gifts of descendants and the promised land are inseparable.

Abram seems almost resigned to the fallback measure offered to childless couples. According to the ancient custom, the barren couple would adopt a slave to care for them in their old age and assure a proper burial. After their death the adopted servant would become their principal heir (verses 2–3). Yet, God emphatically assured Abram not only that he would have a child as an heir, but that his offspring would be innumerable (verse 5). To impress on Abram the enormity of this gift, God invited him to contemplate the star-studded night sky: "So shall your descendants be" (verse 5). Abram would have multitudes of offspring by natural birth, complemented by countless children joined to his lineage by faith.

God seals the promise of land by making a covenant with Abram. Covenants were common in the ancient world for defining and sealing various types of relationships. The covenant between God and Abram contained the basic elements of ancient covenants: the identification of the one initiating the covenant, a statement of the history of the two parties entering the covenant, the blessings provided through the relationship (verse 7), and the ceremony of ratifying the covenant (verses 9–21). In this mysterious ritual of "cutting" the covenant, the animals to be sacrificed are cut in two (verse 10), and the one making the covenant passes between the pieces to solemnly seal the covenant. The ritual expresses the conviction that the parties will suffer the same fate as the animals should they fail to keep the covenant (Jer 34:18). Here God, represented by the flaming torch, passes between the sundered animals making a unilateral, unconditional covenant with Abram (verse 17).

The connecting link between God's promises of descendants and land is Abram's faith: "He believed the Lord; and the Lord reckoned it to him as righteousness" (verse 6). Faith is not defined here; rather the reader is shown what faith is through Abram. He put his full trust in God, even when that trust seemed unwarranted, and thus became the model of faith for us all.

Reflection and discussion

- Why do I need to hear God's words, "Do not be afraid"? Why are fears and doubts a necessary part of growing in faith?

- When have I found it most difficult to trust in God? Am I willing to trust God completely?

- What are the promises God has offered to me? In what way does my confidence in God give hope to my life?

- How would my life be different if I trusted in God completely? What can I do to begin living that kind of life today?

Prayer

God my Shield, I believe that you are my protector and the source of all that I need. Help me to look to Abram as my model of faith. Assist me that I might trust completely in you, even when your promises to me seem distant and doubtful.

The angel of the Lord also said to Hagar, "I will so greatly multiply your offspring that they cannot be counted for multitude." And the angel of the Lord said to her, "Now you have conceived and shall bear a son; you shall call him Ishmael." GENESIS 16:10–11

Sarai Offers Hagar to Bear a Child

GENESIS 16:1–16 1*Now Sarai, Abram's wife, bore him no children. She had*
an Egyptian slave-girl whose name was Hagar, 2*and Sarai said to Abram, "You*
see that the Lord has prevented me from bearing children; go in to my slave-girl;
it may be that I shall obtain children by her." And Abram listened to the voice of
Sarai. 3*So, after Abram had lived ten years in the land of Canaan, Sarai, Abram's*
wife, took Hagar the Egyptian, her slave-girl, and gave her to her husband Abram
as a wife. 4*He went in to Hagar, and she conceived; and when she saw that she had*
conceived, she looked with contempt on her mistress. 5*Then Sarai said to Abram,*
"May the wrong done to me be on you! I gave my slave-girl to your embrace, and
when she saw that she had conceived, she looked on me with contempt. May the
Lord judge between you and me!" 6*But Abram said to Sarai, "Your slave-girl is in*
your power; do to her as you please." Then Sarai dealt harshly with her, and she
ran away from her.

7*The angel of the Lord found her by a spring of water in the wilderness, the*
spring on the way to Shur. 8*And he said, "Hagar, slave-girl of Sarai, where have*
you come from and where are you going?" She said, "I am running away from my
mistress Sarai." 9*The angel of the Lord said to her, "Return to your mistress, and*
submit to her." 10*The angel of the Lord also said to her, "I will so greatly multiply*

your offspring that they cannot be counted for multitude." [11]*And the angel of the Lord said to her,*

"Now you have conceived and shall bear a son;
you shall call him Ishmael,
for the Lord has given heed to your affliction.
[12]*He shall be a wild ass of a man,*
with his hand against everyone,
and everyone's hand against him;
and he shall live at odds with all his kin."

[13]*So she named the Lord who spoke to her, "You are El-roi"; for she said, "Have I really seen God and remained alive after seeing him?"* [14]*Therefore the well was called Beer-lahai-roi; it lies between Kadesh and Bered.*

[15]*Hagar bore Abram a son; and Abram named his son, whom Hagar bore, Ishmael.* [16]*Abram was eighty-six years old when Hagar bore him Ishmael.*

Ten years had elapsed since Abram left Haran with the promise that he would become a great nation (verse 3). The hopes of Abram and Sarai to bear a child reached a critical level of frustration. In desperation, Sarai took the initiative to give Abram an heir and to build their family. She suggested to Abram that he father a child by her Egyptian servant, Hagar (verse 2). The practice of an infertile wife offering a surrogate to her husband was common practice in the ancient Middle East.

Yet, Sarai's well-intended act created a triangle of trouble. The difference between the two women was striking. Sarai was from Abram's tribe, a beautiful but aging woman, free but barren. Hagar was a foreigner, young with the exotic look of an Egyptian, a slave-girl and fertile. Sarai had underestimated her vulnerability to that most unbearable of human emotions: jealousy.

Abram agreed to his wife's plan, and when Abram slept with Hagar, she immediately conceived (verse 4). When Sarai's plan comes to fruition, her selflessness deteriorates into angry accusations against her husband and cruelty toward Hagar. We do not know the details of Sarai's harsh treatment of Hagar, but we know it was ruthless enough to cause the pregnant Hagar to flee into the wilderness (verse 6).

Hagar was fleeing in the direction of her homeland when she was met by an angel of God, the first angelic visitation in the biblical literature (verse 7). God's messenger told her to return and submit to her mistress, but he also gave her a series of incredible divine promises. She would have a son whom she was to name Ishmael. His name means "God hears," for indeed God heard her cry for help and hears the needs of the outcasts. Ishmael's nature was compared to that of the wild ass, a sturdy desert animal whose fierce, fleet-footed love of freedom makes it impossible to domesticate (verses 11–12). Most amazingly, God says to Hagar, "I will so multiply your offspring that they cannot be counted for multitude" (verse 10). Ishmael himself was destined to become the father of twelve tribes and of a great nation (25:12–18).

Hagar's relationship with God is unique. She is the only person in the Bible to give a name to God: El-roi, the God whom I have seen, the God who sees me (verse 13). Only God, through his messenger, calls Hagar by name—Abram and Sarai had only called her slave-girl. Although powerless as female, slave, and foreigner, God hears her, calls he by name, and makes her the mother of a great nation.

Returning to Abram's household, she bore Abram a son. Abram named him Ishmael, designating the boy as his own with all the attendant privileges. For the time being, Abram accepted his son as the fulfillment of God's promise.

Reflection and discussion

- What are the feelings that seem to predominate in the hearts of Sarai and Hagar?

- In what ways did Sarah's plan for surrogate motherhood create a triangle of trouble? What allows triangles of trouble to form in relationships and families?

- How does the text demonstrate that Hagar is uniquely blessed by God? What is surprising about these blessings?

- How can I better use my emotions to be more honest with God in prayer and more genuine in my daily actions?

Prayer

Lord, you are the God who truly sees me. You know the emotional conflicts that rage within me: generosity, jealousy, anger, and hope. Help me to trust in your plan for my life and my family.

SUGGESTIONS FOR FACILITATORS, GROUP SESSION 2

1. If there are newcomers who were not present for the first group session, introduce them now.

2. You may want to pray this prayer as a group:
   Most High God, you are the God who truly sees, who sees us and enables us to trust amid life's adversities. Help us overcome our fear of change, confident in your promises and hoping in the future. Help us imitate the dedication of Abraham and Sarah, who endured sacrifices and worked together for their goals. Show us how to live in trusting confidence in you and to know that you provide all that we need, even when your promises seem distant and doubtful.

3. Ask one of the following questions:
   - What was your biggest challenge in Bible study over this past week?
   - What did you learn about yourself this week?

4. Discuss lessons 1 through 6 together. Assuming that group members have read the Scripture and commentary during the week, there is no need to read it aloud. As you review each lesson, you might want to briefly summarize the Scripture passages of each lesson and ask the group what stands out most clearly from the commentary.

5. Choose one or more of the questions for reflection and discussion from each lesson to talk over as a group. You may want to ask group members which question was most challenging or helpful to them as you review each lesson.

6. Keep the discussion moving, but don't rush the discussion in order to complete more questions. Allow time for the questions that provoke the most discussion.

7. Instruct group members to complete lessons 7 through 12 on their own during the six days before the next group meeting. They should write out their own answers to the questions as preparation for next week's group discussion.

8. Conclude by praying aloud together the prayer at the end of lesson 6, or any other prayer you choose.

I will make you exceedingly fruitful; and I will make nations of you, and kings shall come from you. I will establish my covenant between me and you, and your offspring after you throughout their generations, for an everlasting covenant. GENESIS 17:6–7

Ancestor of a Multitude of Nations

GENESIS 17:1–14 1*When Abram was ninety-nine years old, the Lord appeared*
to Abram, and said to him, "I am God Almighty; walk before me, and be blame-
less. 2*And I will make my covenant between me and you, and will make you exceed-*
ingly numerous." 3*Then Abram fell on his face; and God said to him,* 4*"As for me,*
this is my covenant with you: You shall be the ancestor of a multitude of nations.
5*No longer shall your name be Abram, but your name shall be Abraham; for I have*
made you the ancestor of a multitude of nations. 6*I will make you exceedingly fruit-*
ful; and I will make nations of you, and kings shall come from you. 7*I will establish*
my covenant between me and you, and your offspring after you throughout their
generations, for an everlasting covenant, to be God to you and to your offspring
after you. 8*And I will give to you, and to your offspring after you, the land where*
you are now an alien, all the land of Canaan, for a perpetual holding; and I will
be their God."

9*God said to Abraham, "As for you, you shall keep my covenant, you and your*
offspring after you throughout their generations. 10*This is my covenant, which you*
shall keep, between me and you and your offspring after you: Every male among
you shall be circumcised. 11*You shall circumcise the flesh of your foreskins, and it*
shall be a sign of the covenant between me and you. 12*Throughout your generations*

every male among you shall be circumcised when he is eight days old, including the slave born in your house and the one bought with your money from any foreigner who is not of your offspring. [13]*Both the slave born in your house and the one bought with your money must be circumcised. So shall my covenant be in your flesh an everlasting covenant.* [14]*Any uncircumcised male who is not circumcised in the flesh of his foreskin shall be cut off from his people; he has broken my covenant."*

Twenty-four years after Abram left Haran and thirteen years after the birth of Ishmael, God's promises still remained unfulfilled. Again God appeared to Abram, this time identified as God Almighty (in Hebrew, El Shaddai). The word "covenant" appears ten times in these verses, and the covenant is redefined as an "everlasting covenant." In the earlier covenant making (Gen 15), God was the active partner and Abram the passive recipient of God's promises. Here God asks for a commitment from Abram and summons him to be an active partner in the covenant: "Walk before me and be blameless" (verse 1). Abram was to live with an awareness of God's presence and behave with integrity. In an expression of awe and submission to God, Abram fell prostrate with his face to the ground (verse 3).

Through the covenant, Abram will be "the ancestor of a multitude of nations" (verses 4–5). This implies that Abram will be the father of nations other than Israel. Through his son Ishmael and his future son Isaac, Abram will be the father of two great peoples. Furthermore, Abram will generate an increasingly large segment of humanity that looks upon him as its spiritual ancestor. This expanded role for the patriarch is expressed through the expansion of his name, from Abram ("exalted father") to Abraham ("father of multitudes"; verse 5). A change of names in the Bible signifies a change in a person's character or destiny. The results of God's promises and Abraham's fidelity will unfold generation after generation, as Abraham's offspring would grow into "nations" and "kings" who honor God (verses 6–7).

As part of the active response to the divine promises, God commanded that every male of Abraham's household and of his descendants be circumcised as "a sign of the covenant" (verse 11). The practice of circumcising the foreskins of males was a common practice among the peoples of the ancient Middle East. Abraham needed no explanation or instruction. Yet among other peoples the practice was almost always associated with puberty and preparation for marriage. By commanding circumcision on the eighth day after birth, God fundamentally transformed its meaning. It became the sign and seal of trust in God's promises and entrance into the covenant. As a physical and permanent mark "in the flesh," circumcision symbolized the bearer's enduring, irrevocable commitment to the covenant with God (verses 12–13).

Reflection and discussion

- In what aspect of my life have I had to wait a long time for the fulfillment of God's promises? Is there a value in waiting?

- In what ways has Abraham become the ancestor of "a multitude of nations" (verse 4)? What are the challenges today among the descendants of Abraham in keeping this covenant with God?

- If circumcision is no longer required in the Christian tradition for initiation into the covenant, what is now required (see Gal 5:6)?

Prayer

God Almighty, you have invited me to walk in your presence. Give me the patience to wait for the fulfillment of your pledges. Give me the grace to leave a legacy for future generations.

LESSON 8  **SESSION 3**

Abraham fell on his face and laughed, and said to himself, "Can a child be born to a man who is a hundred years old? Can Sarah, who is ninety years old, bear a child?" GENESIS 17:17

God Promises a Son to Sarah

GENESIS 17:15–27 15*God said to Abraham, "As for Sarah your wife, you shall*
not call her Sarai, but Sarah shall be her name. 16*I will bless her, and moreover I*
will give you a son by her. I will bless her, and she shall give rise to nations; kings
of peoples shall come from her." 17*Then Abraham fell on his face and laughed, and*
said to himself, "Can a child be born to a man who is a hundred years old? Can
Sarah, who is ninety years old, bear a child?" 18*And Abraham said to God, "O that*
Ishmael might live in your sight!" 19*God said, "No, but your wife Sarah shall bear*
you a son, and you shall name him Isaac. I will establish my covenant with him as
an everlasting covenant for his offspring after him. 20*As for Ishmael, I have heard*
you; I will bless him and make him fruitful and exceedingly numerous; he shall be
the father of twelve princes, and I will make him a great nation. 21*But my covenant*
I will establish with Isaac, whom Sarah shall bear to you at this season next year."
22*And when he had finished talking with him, God went up from Abraham.*

23*Then Abraham took his son Ishmael and all the slaves born in his house*
or bought with his money, every male among the men of Abraham's house, and
he circumcised the flesh of their foreskins that very day, as God had said to him.
24*Abraham was ninety-nine years old when he was circumcised in the flesh of his*
foreskin. 25*And his son Ishmael was thirteen years old when he was circumcised in*
the flesh of his foreskin. 26*That very day Abraham and his son Ishmael were cir-*

cumcised; [27] and all the men of his house, slaves born in the house and those bought with money from a foreigner, were circumcised with him.

As God continues to reveal his plan, Sarai, too, is given a new name, Sarah, signifying her new destiny. God will end her infertility and give her a son. No longer would she be a barren woman; she would be the mother of nations, and kings of different peoples would come from her (verses 15–16).

Abraham was so bowled over by God's incredible words that he broke out laughing (verse 17). We are not told whether Abraham's laugh was from surprise, skepticism, mockery, or joy. Perhaps it was a mixture of all of these, the spontaneous laughter that seeks to avoid being overwhelmed by a confusing cacophony of sudden feelings. The blessing given to Sarah seemed impossible, so Abraham tries to redirect God's attention to Ishmael (verse 18). Hadn't this already been settled? Wasn't Ishmael the heir to the covenant? God assured Abraham that Ishmael would indeed be blessed: he would be the father of twelve princes who would become a great nation (verse 20). But Sarah's son, Isaac, will inherit the covenant.

The name Isaac comes from the Hebrew root for "laughter." Every time Abraham would hear his son's name in the future, he would be reminded of God's incredible, laughable ways. After Abraham had waited for so many years for Sarah to have a child, hoping against the evidence, God asked him to believe for just one more year (verse 21). Isaac, forevermore, would represent the triumph of God's power over human limitations and doubt.

Immediately Abraham obeyed God, circumcising Ishmael, all males of his household and among his servants, and even himself, at age ninety-nine (verses 23–27). Through the ritual of circumcision, the covenant would be renewed in each new generation. By performing the rite of circumcision, each child's father acknowledged God's role in the conception and birth of his son, renewing his own covenant with God and marking the starting point of his child's spiritual journey.

The fact that only men bear the sign of the covenant on their bodies should not be viewed as evidence that women have an inferior relationship to God's covenant. A woman's entire body is involved in the conception, birth, and nursing of a child, linking her to her mother and her children and affirming her connection with the Creator. Men have a much more tenuous connection to the mystery of bringing forth new life. The mark of circumcision creates the awareness that a man's sexuality is central to his spiritual identity. The ritual intensifies men's connections to their fathers and their sons, and it heightens their sense of responsibility to raise their children in God's path and to play a personal role in their children's upbringing.

In the Christian tradition, the ancestral rite of circumcision illuminates the practice of baptism. Like circumcision for the Jewish people, baptism is an entrance into a new life and signifies loyalty to a community. The Jewish sign of the covenant became the model for the life of Christian faith through baptism, "a spiritual circumcision," "the circumcision of Christ" (Col 2:11–13).

Reflection and discussion

- What emotions might Abraham have felt when told that he and Sarah would have a son? What caused Abraham's laughter?

- Why is Isaac's name so appropriate? Do I ever associate laughter with God's revealing presence and sacred events?

Prayer

God of Abraham and Sarah, you are eternally faithful to your people. The wonders you work for us are amazing. Help me to trust you when I am besieged by doubts and fears about the future.

Abraham looked up and saw three men standing near him. When he saw them, he ran from the tent entrance to meet them, and bowed down to the ground. GENESIS 18:2

The Aged Sarah Laughs at God's Promise

GENESIS 18:1–15 [1]*The Lord appeared to Abraham by the oaks of Mamre, as he sat at the entrance of his tent in the heat of the day.* [2]*He looked up and saw three men standing near him. When he saw them, he ran from the tent entrance to meet them, and bowed down to the ground.* [3]*He said, "My lord, if I find favor with you, do not pass by your servant.* [4]*Let a little water be brought, and wash your feet, and rest yourselves under the tree.* [5]*Let me bring a little bread, that you may refresh yourselves, and after that you may pass on—since you have come to your servant." So they said, "Do as you have said."* [6]*And Abraham hastened into the tent to Sarah, and said, "Make ready quickly three measures of choice flour, knead it, and make cakes."* [7]*Abraham ran to the herd, and took a calf, tender and good, and gave it to the servant, who hastened to prepare it.* [8]*Then he took curds and milk and the calf that he had prepared, and set it before them; and he stood by them under the tree while they ate.*

[9]*They said to him, "Where is your wife Sarah?" And he said, "There, in the tent."* [10]*Then one said, "I will surely return to you in due season, and your wife Sarah shall have a son." And Sarah was listening at the tent entrance behind him.* [11]*Now Abraham and Sarah were old, advanced in age; it had ceased to be with Sarah after the manner of women.* [12]*So Sarah laughed to herself, saying, "After I have grown old, and my husband is old, shall I have pleasure?"* [13]*The Lord said to Abraham, "Why did Sarah laugh, and say, 'Shall I indeed bear a child, now that*

I am old?' [14]Is anything too wonderful for the Lord? At the set time I will return to you, in due season, and Sarah shall have a son." [15]But Sarah denied, saying, "I did not laugh"; for she was afraid. He said, "Oh yes, you did laugh."

One of the worst casualties of our fast-paced, media-driven culture is the ancient virtue of hospitality. We are losing the art of opening our homes in welcome, graciously attending to the needs of guests, and leisurely sharing meals with others. In the biblical world such graciousness was an honored virtue. The rabbis taught that we draw closest to God not through isolated prayer or sacrificial worship but through personally tending to the everyday needs of others. As the Talmud says, "Hospitality to wayfarers is greater than welcoming the Divine Presence."

Abraham's tent, set in the shade of the oak trees at Mamre, was a hospitable place for travelers. Abraham honored his three guests by offering them a place of rest and refreshment in the noonday heat. His openhearted cordiality knew no bounds. Offering to bring his guests "a little bread," he prepared a feast for them. Bread made of finest flour, curds and milk, and a choice, tender calf made a first-rate spread to place before his guests.

Apparently Abraham does not, at first, think there is anything extraordinary about these three travelers. He rather responds in character to these strangers, demonstrating that he recognizes the presence of God in everyone he meets. The narrator, however, clues in the reader from the beginning that this is a divine visit (verse 1). It is only when the strangers ask about Sarah by name and reveal the extraordinary news of her maternity that there are any clues that Abraham has been entertaining messengers from God (verses 9–10).

Listening from inside the tent, Sarah hears that by this time next year she will have a son. She was so flabbergasted at the silliness of the message that she laughs to herself (verse 12). She wonders how she and old Abe can possibly experience sexual pleasure and conceive a child. Like Abraham in the previous scene (17:17), Sarah laughs because she doesn't know how else to respond to a suggestion that seems so absurd. Yet, when challenged about her laughter by the messenger, Sarah denied laughing because she is embarrassed and afraid (verse 15). The name of her son, Isaac ("he laughs"), will continually remind her of the unpredictable, even humorous ways that God keeps his promises.

The key question of the passage, however, is not about laughter but about the astonishing ways of God: "Is anything too wonderful for the Lord?" (verse 14). The question really is an invitation to faith. Is God's power limited to our expectations of life, or can we dare to believe that God will keep his astounding promises to us? Faith is not a reasonable act that fits into the normal scheme of life but rather the ability to put our trust in what sometimes seems laughable.

Reflection and discussion

- What does this scene by the oaks of Mamre teach me about hospitality? How can I express the art of hospitality?

- The Letter to the Hebrews says: "Do not neglect to show hospitality to strangers, for by doing that some have entertained angels without knowing it" (13:2). What does this verse mean to me?

- "Is anything too wonderful for the Lord?" How do I respond to this question? What is the most wonderful promise God has made to me?

Prayer

Lord God, every person is created in your image and contains a spark of your divine life. Help me to see your face in the people I meet, especially in the wayfarer and the stranger.

Then Abraham came near and said, "Will you indeed sweep away the righteous with the wicked? Suppose there are fifty righteous within the city; will you then sweep away the place and not forgive it for the fifty righteous who are in it?" GENESIS 18:23–24

Abraham Intercedes for Sodom

GENESIS 18:16–33 *[16]Then the men set out from there, and they looked toward*
Sodom; and Abraham went with them to set them on their way. [17]The Lord said,
"Shall I hide from Abraham what I am about to do, [18]seeing that Abraham shall
become a great and mighty nation, and all the nations of the earth shall be blessed
in him? [19]No, for I have chosen him, that he may charge his children and his house-
hold after him to keep the way of the Lord by doing righteousness and justice; so
that the Lord may bring about for Abraham what he has promised him." [20]Then
the Lord said, "How great is the outcry against Sodom and Gomorrah and how
very grave their sin! [21]I must go down and see whether they have done altogether
according to the outcry that has come to me; and if not, I will know."

[22]So the men turned from there, and went toward Sodom, while Abraham
remained standing before the Lord. [23]Then Abraham came near and said, "Will
you indeed sweep away the righteous with the wicked? [24]Suppose there are fifty
righteous within the city; will you then sweep away the place and not forgive it
for the fifty righteous who are in it? [25]Far be it from you to do such a thing, to slay
the righteous with the wicked, so that the righteous fare as the wicked! Far be that
from you! Shall not the Judge of all the earth do what is just?" [26]And the Lord said,
"If I find at Sodom fifty righteous in the city, I will forgive the whole place for their

sake." [27]*Abraham answered, "Let me take it upon myself to speak to the Lord, I who am but dust and ashes.* [28]*Suppose five of the fifty righteous are lacking? Will you destroy the whole city for lack of five?" And he said, "I will not destroy it if I find forty-five there."* [29]*Again he spoke to him, "Suppose forty are found there." He answered, "For the sake of forty I will not do it."* [30]*Then he said, "Oh do not let the Lord be angry if I speak. Suppose thirty are found there." He answered, "I will not do it, if I find thirty there."* [31]*He said, "Let me take it upon myself to speak to the Lord. Suppose twenty are found there." He answered, "For the sake of twenty I will not destroy it."* [32]*Then he said, "Oh do not let the Lord be angry if I speak just once more. Suppose ten are found there." He answered, "For the sake of ten I will not destroy it."* [33]*And the Lord went his way, when he had finished speaking to Abraham; and Abraham returned to his place.*

The divine messengers continue their journey, looking toward Sodom, their next destination. Abraham, always the hospitable host, walks along with them to see them on their way (verse 16). God wonders if he should tell Abraham about the mission of his messengers: to determine whether or not divine judgment should be executed on the sinful cities of Sodom and Gomorrah (verses 17, 20–21). In deciding to inform Abraham about the mission of his messengers, God reiterated that "all the nations of the earth shall be blessed in him" (verse 18; 12:3). God's message reveals the divine will that Abraham and his descendants mediate for other peoples, especially those under judgment, and in that way become a source of blessings for other nations. As bearer of God's promises toward all peoples, Abraham and his progeny would have the privilege of interceding for the sake of others in the interactive relationship God desires between himself and human beings.

The sin and punishment of Sodom and Gomorrah have transformed the names of those cities into permanent reminders of human wickedness and divine judgment. God describes his judgment of the city with two exclamations: "How great is the outcry against Sodom and Gomorrah and how very grave their sin!" (verse 20). An "outcry" in the Bible is usually a plea by those suffering from oppression, a cry to heaven with hopes that God will rescue them. The sin, it seems, is social corruption: an arrogant disregard for basic human rights and a cynical insensitivity to the sufferings of others (Jer 23:14; Ezek 16:49). God was going there to see if the volume of the outcry corresponded with the reality of the oppression.

Abraham stands before God to plead on behalf of the pagan people of Sodom. He decides to appeal for God to save the wicked city of Sodom based on the merits of an innocent minority. Thinking that God must be a harsh and calculating judge like the gods of the surrounding nations, Abraham prepares to plead and bargain with God. Abraham first chooses the number fifty as his bartering figure: save the city on behalf of fifty righteous people (verse 24). He purposely chose a low number, thinking that in the style of a typical bargaining, God would choose a much higher number, and then they would meet somewhere in the middle. But Abraham's strategy is undone by God's immediate acceptance of his offer. Lowering the offer to forty-five, forty, thirty, twenty, and finally ten, Abraham discovers that God is far more merciful than he had imagined.

Although Sodom is destroyed (Gen 19), apparently because not even ten righteous people could be found there, God does save the family of Lot. Through his experience Abraham learned from God "the way of the Lord" (verse 19), the way of justice, righteousness, and mercy that characterizes God's action among his creation. God does not judge by the usual moralism, in which people simply receive their due. God in not a score-keeper, always ready to pounce and punish; rather God is far more ready to forgive and to celebrate the goodness of a few. In this way, Abraham is able to teach God's way to his posterity. As the Talmud observes: "Whoever is merciful to his fellow human beings is without doubt of the children of our father Abraham; whoever is unmerciful to his fellow beings certainly cannot be of the children of Abraham our father." God wants his people to boldly appeal to him, to plea for others who are hurting or in sin. When God is approached with genuine concern and pure motives, he is moved by intercessory prayer.

Reflection and discussion

- What are the pros and cons of this type of negotiating with God? In what way does God challenge Abraham's assumptions about the way God works?

- What is most surprising about God's response to Abraham's bargaining? How does Abraham's experience challenge me to doubt and question my routine ways of thinking about God?

- Abraham's courageous intercession for the people of Sodom teaches us not to be passive spectators in the face of the world's challenges, but to intercede with active compassion. In what ways am I able to intercede for other people before God?

Prayer

God of justice and mercy, you demonstrate that you are always ready to forgive and welcome us back to you. Teach me your ways so that I can make your compassion known to others. Give me an active concern for the people of our world.

LESSON 11  SESSION 3

**Abimelech took sheep and oxen, and male and female slaves,
and gave them to Abraham, and restored his wife Sarah to him.
Abimelech said, "My land is before you; settle where it pleases you."**
GENESIS 20:14–15

Abraham and Sarah at Gerar

GENESIS 20:1–18 [1]*From there Abraham journeyed toward the region of the*
Negeb, and settled between Kadesh and Shur. While residing in Gerar as an alien,
[2]*Abraham said of his wife Sarah, "She is my sister." And King Abimelech of Gerar*
sent and took Sarah.

[3]*But God came to Abimelech in a dream by night, and said to him, "You are*
about to die because of the woman whom you have taken; for she is a married
woman." [4]*Now Abimelech had not approached her; so he said, "Lord, will you*
destroy an innocent people? [5]*Did he not himself say to me, 'She is my sister'? And*
she herself said, 'He is my brother.' I did this in the integrity of my heart and the
innocence of my hands." [6]*Then God said to him in the dream, "Yes, I know that you*
did this in the integrity of your heart; furthermore it was I who kept you from sin-
ning against me. Therefore I did not let you touch her. [7]*Now then, return the man's*
wife; for he is a prophet, and he will pray for you and you shall live. But if you do
not restore her, know that you shall surely die, you and all that are yours."

[8]*So Abimelech rose early in the morning, and called all his servants and told*
them all these things; and the men were very much afraid. [9]*Then Abimelech called*
Abraham, and said to him, "What have you done to us? How have I sinned against
you, that you have brought such great guilt on me and my kingdom? You have done

things to me that ought not to be done." [10]*And Abimelech said to Abraham, "What were you thinking of, that you did this thing?"* [11]*Abraham said, "I did it because I thought, There is no fear of God at all in this place, and they will kill me because of my wife.* [12]*Besides, she is indeed my sister, the daughter of my father but not the daughter of my mother; and she became my wife.* [13]*And when God caused me to wander from my father's house, I said to her, 'This is the kindness you must do me: at every place to which we come, say of me, He is my brother.'"* [14]*Then Abimelech took sheep and oxen, and male and female slaves, and gave them to Abraham, and restored his wife Sarah to him.* [15]*Abimelech said, "My land is before you; settle where it pleases you."* [16]*To Sarah he said, "Look, I have given your brother a thousand pieces of silver; it is your exoneration before all who are with you; you are completely vindicated."* [17]*Then Abraham prayed to God; and God healed Abimelech, and also healed his wife and female slaves so that they bore children.* [18]*For the Lord had closed fast all the wombs of the house of Abimelech because of Sarah, Abraham's wife.*

Abraham and Sarah resumed their wanderings through the promised land, traveling to its southernmost limits, the oasis of Kadesh and the Egyptian fortress of Shur. They then entered the royal city of Gerar, perhaps for the purpose of trade in the city. Fearing for his own life, Abraham again resorted to the strategy of introducing Sarah as his sister, the same ploy he had used in Egypt (verse 2; 12:10–20). Again, Sarah is taken into the king's harem but is saved from dishonor by God's intervention.

We are not told why King Abimelech took Sarah into the royal family. The Jewish midrash comments that with the promise of a child, God had restored not only Sarah's childbearing capacity but her youthful beauty as well. It is quite possible, however, that Abimelech wanted to form an economically advantageous alliance with Abraham through marriage to his "sister."

God then revealed to Abimelech in a dream that he was under the threat of death because of his abduction of a married woman (verse 3). But, defending his innocence, Abimelech argued on two grounds: he had not "approached her," another way of saying he did not have sexual relations with her, and he was not aware of her married status, since he had been told that she was Abraham's sister (verses 4–5).

Abimelech's dialogue with God revolves on the theme of God's justice—whether God would destroy innocent people—as does Abraham's dialogue with God about the city of Sodom (verses 4–7; 18:16–33). The king of Gerar and his people are saved through the prayers of Abraham (verses 7, 17), just as Lot was saved. In both narratives, Abraham was the intercessor before God on behalf of others. Here God describes Abraham as a "prophet," the first use of this term in the Bible. In this role, Abraham is not only a spokesperson for God, but a mediator between God and other people. He prays that Abimelech might be healed and live.

Deeply affected by his dream, the king summoned his officials, who are fearful about the matter (verse 8). Confronted by Abimelech, Abraham offers a feeble explanation (verses 9–13). Though portrayed as far less than righteous, Abraham nevertheless emerges with his authority and his riches enhanced, and the king tells him he may dwell wherever he wishes (verses 14–16). The preeminence of Abraham rests not on his own virtues but on God's promise.

Reflection and discussion

- Does God still reveal his will to people in dreams? What dream has taught me something about myself and what God might want for me?

- In what ways does this passage show Abraham to be less than virtuous? How does Abimelech act more honorably than Abraham in this account?

- In what aspects of this account do I most identify with Abraham? Doubting God's promises? Needing to be rescued from my own mistakes? Making the same mistakes again?

- In what ways does this passage show that God's grace overcomes human frailty and faithlessness? How have I seen God's grace working in this way in my own life?

- In what way does my experience of God's merciful pardon lead me to want to forgive others? How can I forgive someone today?

Prayer

Mighty God, for the sake of your promises you heal our human faults and infidelity. Show me how to be an intercessor for others, praying to you for their healing and forgiveness.

And Sarah said, "Who would ever have said to Abraham that Sarah would nurse children? Yet I have borne him a son in his old age."
GENESIS 21:7

Laughing with Sarah at Isaac's Birth

GENESIS 21:1–7 *[1]The Lord dealt with Sarah as he had said, and the Lord did for Sarah as he had promised. [2]Sarah conceived and bore Abraham a son in his old age, at the time of which God had spoken to him. [3]Abraham gave the name Isaac to his son whom Sarah bore him. [4]And Abraham circumcised his son Isaac when he was eight days old, as God had commanded him. [5]Abraham was a hundred years old when his son Isaac was born to him. [6]Now Sarah said, "God has brought laughter for me; everyone who hears will laugh with me." [7]And she said, "Who would ever have said to Abraham that Sarah would nurse children? Yet I have borne him a son in his old age."*

God keeps his word. If there is any message that comes through clearly in the Abraham narratives, it is that God is faithful in keeping his promises: "The Lord did for Sarah as he had promised" (verse 1). But God's promises are not delivered according to our timetable. The text tells us that Abraham was a hundred years old when his son Isaac was born (verse 5). A full quarter century had passed since he first heard God's call promising him innumerable descendants. The stance of the believer, then, in awaiting the fulfillment of God's promises after the example of Abraham, is patient expectation.

The birth of Isaac is the culmination of a history of obstacles and disappointments. The Abraham narratives up to this point have described a series of crises that threatened to make the fulfillment of divine promises impossible. Yet, the brief narrative of Isaac's birth describes matter-of-factly that indeed God's word has come to fruition. The child's birth is the resolution of all the anxious waiting, worries, and doubts. This brief passage is the perfect portrait and ideal model for God's faithfulness. Each detail describes how the expectations of the previous narratives find their completion in Isaac's birth. Sarah bore Abraham a son according to the schedule the divine messengers had relayed, "at the time of which God has spoken to him" (verse 2; 18:14). Abraham named his son Isaac, as God had previously directed him (verse 3; 17:19), and he circumcised his son on the eighth day after his birth, just as God had decreed (verse 4; 17:12). Isaac is the first person circumcised according to God's timetable, after seven days of life, emphasizing Isaac's role as the true heir to the covenant.

This newborn son is so appropriately named: Isaac—he laughs. Sarah says, "God has brought laughter to me" (verse 6). Laughter seems the appropriate response to a newness that cannot be reasonably explained. Through his word and promise, God has broken the sullen grip of barrenness and hopelessness. The promised son is a work of pure grace—an unearned, undeserved gift. Sarah's earlier laugh of embarrassed skepticism (18:12–15) now becomes joyous, unrestrained laughter. It is a contagious laughter that will spread to all who hear the news of Isaac's birth. Sarah is glad that everyone who hears will laugh along with her.

Reflection and discussion

- Why is "Laughter" such a perfect name for Sarah's child?

- In what ways does the narrative reveal that God is both faithful and unpredictable? How does the text describe the relationship between divine and human faithfulness?

- Why might God delay the fulfillment of his promises to us? What is the longest I have had to wait for God to act? Have I ever seen advantages in relying on God's timetable rather than my own?

- In what ways is Sarah's laughter contagious? When have I experienced the presence of God through laughter?

Prayer

Lord God, I am grateful for the unearned gifts you have given me. Give me the gift of faith so that I may trust in you completely, the gift of hope that I may look to the future with confidence, and the gift of laughter that I may rejoice in your grace.

SUGGESTIONS FOR FACILITATORS, GROUP SESSION 3

1. Welcome group members and ask if there are any announcements anyone would like to make.

2. You may want to pray this prayer as a group:
   God of Abraham and Sarah, you show us that every person is created in your image and contains a spark of your divine life. Because you have demonstrated that you are always ready to forgive and welcome your people back to you, help us to trust you when we are besieged by doubts and fears about the future. Show us how to be intercessors for others, praying to you for their healing and forgiveness. Give us an active concern for the people of your world so that we may make your compassion known to others.

3. Ask one of the following questions:
   - Which image from the lessons this week stands out most memorably to you?
   - What is the most important lesson you learned through your study this week?

4. Discuss lessons 7 through 12. Choose one or more of the questions for reflection and discussion from each lesson to discuss as a group. You may want to ask group members which question was most challenging or helpful to them as you review each lesson.

5. Remember that there are no definitive answers for these discussion questions. The insights of group members will add to the understanding of all. None of these questions require an expert.

6. After talking about each lesson, instruct group members to complete lessons 13 through 18 on their own during the six days before the next group meeting. They should write out their own answers to the questions as preparation for next week's group discussion.

7. Ask the group if anyone is having any particular problems with the Bible study during the week. You may want to share advice and encouragement within the group.

8. Conclude by praying aloud together the prayer at the end of one of the lessons discussed. You may add to the prayer based on the sharing that has occurred in the group.

LESSON 13  SESSION 4

"Do not be afraid; for God has heard the voice of the boy where he is. Come, lift up the boy and hold him fast with your hand, for I will make a great nation of him." GENESIS 21:17–18

Banishment of Hagar and Ishmael

GENESIS 21:8–21 8*The child grew, and was weaned; and Abraham made a*
great feast on the day that Isaac was weaned. 9*But Sarah saw the son of Hagar the*
Egyptian, whom she had borne to Abraham, playing with her son Isaac. 10*So she*
said to Abraham, "Cast out this slave woman with her son; for the son of this slave
woman shall not inherit along with my son Isaac." 11*The matter was very distressing*
to Abraham on account of his son. 12*But God said to Abraham, "Do not be distressed*
because of the boy and because of your slave woman; whatever Sarah says to you, do
as she tells you, for it is through Isaac that offspring shall be named for you. 13*As for*
the son of the slave woman, I will make a nation of him also, because he is your off-
spring." 14*So Abraham rose early in the morning, and took bread and a skin of water,*
and gave it to Hagar, putting it on her shoulder, along with the child, and sent her
away. And she departed, and wandered about in the wilderness of Beer-sheba.

15*When the water in the skin was gone, she cast the child under one of the bushes.*
16*Then she went and sat down opposite him a good way off, about the distance of a*
bowshot; for she said, "Do not let me look on the death of the child." And as she sat
opposite him, she lifted up her voice and wept. 17*And God heard the voice of the boy;*
and the angel of God called to Hagar from heaven, and said to her, "What troubles
you, Hagar? Do not be afraid; for God has heard the voice of the boy where he is.
18*Come, lift up the boy and hold him fast with your hand, for I will make a great*

nation of him." [19]*Then God opened her eyes and she saw a well of water. She went, and filled the skin with water, and gave the boy a drink.* [20]*God was with the boy, and he grew up; he lived in the wilderness, and became an expert with the bow.* [21]*He lived in the wilderness of Paran; and his mother got a wife for him from the land of Egypt.*

The joyful laughter of Isaac's birth is soon overshadowed by the sad family discord that began on the feast of Isaac's weaning. Because infant mortality was so high in Canaanite culture, families celebrated a child's survival of infancy and the beginning of childhood's next stage by throwing a feast at the child's weaning, usually around the age of two or three (verse 8). The conflict began when Sarah saw the son of Hagar "playing" with her son, Isaac (verse 9). The word translated here as "playing" can also mean "mocking," "making fun of," or "fooling around." Considering that Ishmael was the older brother of Isaac, such conduct should not be surprising.

Sarah became protective when she saw Ishmael's behavior, and she pleaded with Abraham to banish "this slave woman and her son" (verse 10). Legally it seems that Ishmael held the inheritance rights of Abraham's firstborn son. The key to understanding Sarah's demand is the legal clause that allows a father to grant freedom to a slave woman and the children she has borne him, in which case they give up their share of inherited property (see Judg 11:1–3). Sarah is insisting that Abraham release Hagar and Ishmael so that they forfeit any inheritance.

Abraham was in great distress over the emotional conflict between fatherly love for his firstborn and loyalty to his beloved wife (verse 11). Yet God prompted Abraham to agree to Sarah's demands based on two assurances: first, God tells Abraham that his line will continue through Isaac, and second, God has other plans in mind for Ishmael, plans that will give him a great future (verses 12–13). So reluctantly Abraham packed food and water for Hagar and sent her away with Ishmael the next day (verse 14).

Though Hagar and Ishmael were presumably heading in the direction of Hagar's native Egypt, she lost her way and began to wander frantically in the wilderness. When the water was consumed and they were in danger of death in the desert, Hagar and her son cried out to God in desperation. God heard their cry and sent a word of hope through the voice of a divine messenger.

The angel instructed her to lift the boy up because God was going to make him into "a great nation" (verse 18).

The stories of the two sons are juxtaposed. As in the parable of the prodigal son told by Jesus, the older son pleases his father, obeys the rules, and deserves honor, but the younger son is celebrated. God honors both sons of Abraham, and the text does not force us to choose one or the other. God remembers both of Abraham's children. While Isaac is celebrated, God remembers Ishmael, offering him water in the wilderness and assurances of a noble future.

Reflection and discussion

- What do Sarah, Hagar, and Abraham demonstrate about maternal and paternal instincts?

- What are some of the emotional conflicts adults feel between love for their children and love for their spouse? In what ways are these emotions intensified and complicated in blended families that include children, stepchildren, spouses, and ex-spouses?

- What dos and don'ts can I learn from this episode for achieving the sensitive balance required in blended families today?

Prayer

God of our fathers and mothers, you called Abraham, Hagar, and Sarah to be the patriarch and matriarchs of great peoples and nations. Help me to live a life worthy of the great legacy I have been given by my ancestors, and help me to pass on my faith to the next generation.

LESSON 14  SESSION 4

He said, "These seven ewe lambs you shall accept from my hand, in order that you may be a witness for me that I dug this well." Therefore that place was called Beer-sheba; because there both of them swore an oath. GENESIS 21:30–31

Abraham's Well at Beer-sheba

GENESIS 21:22–34 *22At that time Abimelech, with Phicol the commander of his army, said to Abraham, "God is with you in all that you do; 23now therefore swear to me here by God that you will not deal falsely with me or with my offspring or with my posterity, but as I have dealt loyally with you, you will deal with me and with the land where you have resided as an alien." 24And Abraham said, "I swear it."*

25When Abraham complained to Abimelech about a well of water that Abimelech's servants had seized, 26Abimelech said, "I do not know who has done this; you did not tell me, and I have not heard of it until today." 27So Abraham took sheep and oxen and gave them to Abimelech, and the two men made a covenant. 28Abraham set apart seven ewe lambs of the flock. 29And Abimelech said to Abraham, "What is the meaning of these seven ewe lambs that you have set apart?" 30He said, "These seven ewe lambs you shall accept from my hand, in order that you may be a witness for me that I dug this well." 31Therefore that place was called Beer-sheba; because there both of them swore an oath. 32When they had made a covenant at Beer-sheba, Abimelech, with Phicol the commander of his army, left and returned to the land of the Philistines. 33Abraham planted a tamarisk tree in Beer-sheba, and called there on the name of the Lord, the Everlasting God. 34And Abraham resided as an alien many days in the land of the Philistines.

Now that Abraham is assured of countless descendants through both Ishmael and Isaac, the narratives focus on Abraham's claim on the land. Abimelech, the king of Gerar, sees Abraham's growing prosperity and desires to establish a peaceful relationship with him. Abimelech wants to protect his family, his flocks, and most importantly, access to the wells of the desert. Abraham is shown with a new sense of confidence as his influence widens, and he is depicted here as a desert sheik on par with Abimelech. The king traveled from Gerar to Beer-sheba to speak with Abraham. Abimelech opened the dialogue by paying Abraham the highest compliment: "God is with you in all that you do" (verse 22).

Because Abraham was indeed prospering in every way, just as God had promised him upon leaving Haran, Abimelech wanted to enter a covenant with Abraham. The covenant would include a pact of mutual nonaggression, protecting their children and descendants through the generations (verse 23). Abimelech asked Abraham to swear he would not "deal falsely" with him or his posterity, probably alluding to the way Abraham had deceived him about Sarah (chapter 20). The king also asked Abraham to "deal loyally" with him, as he had acted reliably with Abraham, recalling the way he had acted in settling the episode with Sarah. The covenant between Abimelech and Abraham takes the form of an oral oath, and the keeping of it is based on the two men's sense of honor and their belief that the divine witness to the pledge would punish the oath breaker. The covenant was solemnized as the two men slaughtered animals for a ritual sacrifice (verse 27).

As an example of the new covenant between Abimelech and Abraham, the two men mutually resolved an issue of disputed water rights. Abraham asserted his claim to a well that Abimelech's servants had seized, preventing Abraham from freely watering his herds. Abimelech responded by defending himself from blame, stating his ignorance about the seizure had prevented him from correcting the matter.

Abraham presented Abimelech with seven ewe lambs in gratitude for the king's witness that Abraham had dug the well (verses 28–30). By accepting them as a gift, Abimelech acknowledged Abraham's ownership of the well. Abraham named the place Beer-sheba, which means both "the well of seven" and "the well of the oath." The episode highlights the name Beer-sheba, since the Hebrew word *sheba,* meaning both "seven" and "swear an oath" is artfully woven into the entire passage. Beer-sheba would become the place most closely associated with Abraham.

Reflection and discussion

- What did the number "seven" mean for Abraham and Abimelech? Where else in the Bible does the number "seven" have special significance? Is the number significant in my life of faith?

- Abraham planted a tamarisk tree in Beer-sheba (verse 33), a slow-growing tree with deep roots. Why is the tree an effective memorial for the commitments involved in a covenant?

- The Well of Abraham can still be seen today when visiting Beersheba. Why would a well be such an important possession in the time of Abraham?

Prayer

El Olam, Everlasting God, you committed yourself to your people in the bond of the covenant, and you encourage us to make lasting commitments to others. Keep me faithful to my baptismal promises and to the other covenants I have made.

LESSON 15  SESSION 4

Abraham took the wood of the burnt offering and laid it on his son Isaac, and he himself carried the fire and the knife. So the two of them walked on together. GENESIS 22:6

Abraham's Supreme Test

GENESIS 22:1–8 *1After these things God tested Abraham. He said to him,*
"Abraham!" And he said, "Here I am." 2He said, "Take your son, your only son
Isaac, whom you love, and go to the land of Moriah, and offer him there as a burnt
offering on one of the mountains that I shall show you."
3So Abraham rose early in the morning, saddled his donkey, and took two of
his young men with him, and his son Isaac; he cut the wood for the burnt offering,
and set out and went to the place in the distance that God had shown him. 4On the
third day Abraham looked up and saw the place far away. 5Then Abraham said to
his young men, "Stay here with the donkey; the boy and I will go over there; we will
worship, and then we will come back to you." 6Abraham took the wood of the burnt
offering and laid it on his son Isaac, and he himself carried the fire and the knife. So
the two of them walked on together. 7Isaac said to his father Abraham, "Father!"
And he said, "Here I am, my son." He said, "The fire and the wood are here, but
where is the lamb for a burnt offering?" 8Abraham said, "God himself will provide
the lamb for a burnt offering, my son." So the two of them walked on together.

We have arrived at the climactic episode of Abraham's long life, one of the Bible's most dramatic scenes. God's command to sacrifice Isaac is described as a "test" (verse 1), which is information imparted to the reader but not disclosed to Abraham. The Bible is filled with accounts of God's testing his people. This testing might seem unreasonable in light of our belief that God is all-knowing, but God is always engaged with his people—calling, leading, promising, providing, and yes, testing. God tests to determine who is serious about faith, to identify in whose lives he will fully be God, and to develop in his people certain desirable qualities for the life of faith. Like Job, Abraham is prepared to trust fully the God who gives and who takes away (Job 1:21).

God's first call to Abraham from Haran (12:1–4) and this last call to Abraham to go to Moriah are the two pillars which support the entire structure of Abraham's spiritual odyssey. The command of God is almost identical: "Go…to the land that I will show you" (12:1); "Go to the land of Moriah… on one of the mountains that I will show you" (verse 2). In both calls the enormity of what God asks is heightened by a series of increasingly painful terms with narrowing focus: "your country, your kindred, your father's house" (12:1); "your son, your only son Isaac, whom you love" (verse 2). In the first, Abraham is summoned to relinquish his entire past; in the second, he is called to give up his entire future, the promised son from whom Abraham would have countless descendants.

How does Abraham respond? Was he calm, angry, trusting, miserable, despairing? Did he pass a restless night before he "rose early in the morning" (verse 3)? We can only speculate about Abraham's interior emotions. His preparatory actions are described with a verbal scarcity appropriate to the solemn silence that pervades the scene: he rose, saddled, took, cut the wood, set out and went, looked up and saw. With only the sound of their sandals and the donkey's hooves in the desert sand, the long three-day trek allows time for somber reflection. Abraham could turn back at any time; his will was free; the burden of choice fell squarely on his shoulders. He knows that despite every reasonable impulse within him crying out to defy God's command, he must trustingly "go" once again, proving his faith and confirming his destiny. This is an epic journey.

Nearing the mountain of sacrifice, Abraham told his attendants to wait with the donkey while he and Isaac climb the road to the divinely chosen place. "We will worship, and then we will come back to you" (verse 5). Is Abraham simply trying to conceal from Isaac the true purpose of the journey, or does he harbor a secret hope that indeed they may both return? Abraham took the wood for the sacrifice and laid it on the shoulders of his son (verse 6). Isaac, unaware, carried the wood of his own destruction. "The two of them walked on together" (verses 6–8)—Isaac in unsuspecting innocence and Abraham in unspeakable inner torment.

In the only words between the son and his father, Isaac asks, "The fire and the wood are here, but where is the lamb for a burnt-offering?" (verse 7). Is this penetrating query simply an obvious questions, or, in a culture in which child sacrifice was not unknown, is a suspicion of the dreadful truth beginning to dawn on Isaac? Abraham's trusting words, "God himself will provide the lamb for a burnt-offering" (verse 8), expressed the hope that lay deep within him. Abraham knew that somehow the One who tested was also the One who provided.

Reflection and discussion

- What is most perplexing and shocking about this account for me? What are my unanswered questions?

- What did God really want from Abraham? How can testing help me to know myself better?

- What emotions might Abraham have experienced as he walked up the mountain with Isaac? What do I feel as I read this account?

Prayer

Father, I want to be able to entrust my life to you and to do what you ask of me. Give me the strength to always remain faithful to you and to trust your plan for my life.

"Because you have done this, and have not withheld your son, your only son, I will indeed bless you, and I will make your offspring as numerous as the stars of heaven and as the sand that is on the seashore." GENESIS 22:16–17

The Binding of Isaac

GENESIS 22:9–19 *[9]When they came to the place that God had shown him,*
Abraham built an altar there and laid the wood in order. He bound his son Isaac,
and laid him on the altar, on top of the wood. [10]Then Abraham reached out his
hand and took the knife to kill his son.

[11]But the angel of the Lord called to him from heaven, and said, "Abraham,
Abraham!" And he said, "Here I am." [12]He said, "Do not lay your hand on the
boy or do anything to him; for now I know that you fear God, since you have not
withheld your son, your only son, from me." [13]And Abraham looked up and saw a
ram, caught in a thicket by its horns. Abraham went and took the ram and offered
it up as a burnt offering instead of his son. [14]So Abraham called that place "The
Lord will provide"; as it is said to this day, "On the mount of the Lord it shall
be provided."

[15]The angel of the Lord called to Abraham a second time from heaven, [16]and
said, "By myself I have sworn, says the Lord: Because you have done this, and have
not withheld your son, your only son, [17]I will indeed bless you, and I will make
your offspring as numerous as the stars of heaven and as the sand that is on the
seashore. And your offspring shall possess the gate of their enemies, [18]and by your
offspring shall all the nations of the earth gain blessing for themselves, because you
have obeyed my voice." [19]So Abraham returned to his young men, and they arose
and went together to Beer-sheba; and Abraham lived at Beer-sheba.

The preparations for sacrifice are expressed in the starkest terms: Abraham built an altar, laid the wood upon it, bound his son, laid him on the altar, reached out his hand and took the knife (verses 9–10). There is no dialogue; the anguished grief is beyond words. Is the knife the same instrument Abraham used to circumcise his infant son—an earlier expression of Abraham's trusting commitment to God? Since Abraham was elderly and Isaac was at least old enough to carry wood on his shoulder, surely the boy was strong enough to resist his father. But as Abraham was obedient to God, Isaac was obedient to his father and let himself be bound and placed on the altar.

At the moment Abraham raised his knife to slay his son, God's messenger called out to him and stayed his hand. "Now I know that you fear God, since you have not withheld your son, your only son, from me" (verses 11–12). Abraham's commitment to God had been put to the ultimate test, and he had shown himself wholehearted in his self-surrender to God's will. It was not that God's foreknowledge of Abraham's character was lacking; rather, for Abraham's sake, his inner potential had to be demonstrated in action. Thereby, he became the exemplar of the God-fearing man, the model of genuine faith.

Abraham interprets the fortuitous presence of a ram to mean that God desires a substitute animal sacrifice in place of his son (verse 13). We can't fully imagine the happiness as Isaac and Abraham watched the smoke of the offering ascend to God from the mountain that day. The use of the past tense of the same three verbs as in God's original order—go, take, and offer (verse 2)—indicate that in God's eyes Abraham accomplished what he had set out to do.

Abraham called the place "The Lord will provide" (verse 14), a reminder to all Abraham's descendants that God truly does provide for the needs of those who trust in him (verse 8). Abraham's greatest challenge proves that the God who tests is also the God who provides. Most of us only want a God who provides, but the life of Abraham teaches us that we cannot choose between these two baffling characteristics of God if we want to be people of faith.

Abraham's willingness to offer up his son to God (verse 16) helps us to better understand God's work in his Son, Jesus. God asked Abraham to do what God would do in offering up his only beloved Son on the cross. "He who did not withhold his own Son, but gave him up for us all" (Rom 8:32) is the same God who tested and provided for Abraham. The obedient offering of Abraham strengthened God's covenant with Abraham. The one who had proven faithful would have descendants as numerous as the stars of heaven and the sand of the seashore, and all the nations of the earth would be blessed because Abraham obeyed God's voice (verses 17–18).

Reflection and discussion

- Mount Moriah (verse 2) was identified in later tradition with the temple mount in Jerusalem (2 Chron 3:1). What does this connection with Abraham teach us about the sacrificial worship in the temple?

- What does Abraham demonstrate about his own character through the binding of Isaac? What has God taught me about myself through testing?

- In the New Testament, Paul writes: "God is faithful, and he will not let you be tested beyond your strength, but with the testing he will also provide the way out so that you may be able to endure it" (1 Cor 10:13). How does Abraham's experience demonstrate the truth of Paul's words?

Prayer

God of our ancestors, Abraham, Isaac, and Jacob, you test your servants so that they may develop their faith and be identified as your own. Give me strength in times of testing and assure me that you will provide the way out.

The Hittites answered Abraham, "Hear us, my lord; you are a mighty prince among us. Bury your dead in the choicest of our burial places; none of us will withhold from you any burial ground for burying your dead." GENESIS 23:5–6

Abraham Purchases the Burial Cave at Hebron

GENESIS 23:1–16 *[1]Sarah lived one hundred twenty-seven years; this was the length of Sarah's life. [2]And Sarah died at Kiriath-arba (that is, Hebron) in the land of Canaan; and Abraham went in to mourn for Sarah and to weep for her. [3]Abraham rose up from beside his dead, and said to the Hittites, [4]"I am a stranger and an alien residing among you; give me property among you for a burying place, so that I may bury my dead out of my sight." [5]The Hittites answered Abraham, [6]"Hear us, my lord; you are a mighty prince among us. Bury your dead in the choicest of our burial places; none of us will withhold from you any burial ground for burying your dead." [7]Abraham rose and bowed to the Hittites, the people of the land. [8]He said to them, "If you are willing that I should bury my dead out of my sight, hear me, and entreat for me Ephron son of Zohar, [9]so that he may give me the cave of Machpelah, which he owns; it is at the end of his field. For the full price let him give it to me in your presence as a possession for a burying place." [10]Now Ephron was sitting among the Hittites; and Ephron the Hittite answered Abraham in the hearing of the Hittites, of all who went in at the gate of his city, [11]"No, my lord, hear me; I give you the field, and I give you the cave that is in it; in the presence of my people I give it to you; bury your dead." [12]Then Abraham bowed down before the people of the land. [13]He said to Ephron in the hearing of the people of* *the land, "If you only will listen to me! I will give the price of the field; accept it from me, so that I may bury my dead there."* [14]*Ephron answered Abraham,* [15]*"My lord, listen to me; a piece of land worth four hundred shekels of silver—what is that between you and me? Bury your dead."* [16]*Abraham agreed with Ephron; and Abraham weighed out for Ephron the silver that he had named in the hearing of the Hittites, four hundred shekels of silver, according to the weights current among the merchants.*

There is wonderful freedom that comes with age: finally secure in our identity, less paralyzed by the opinions of others, free to say what we think and feel. Wouldn't it be wonderful if we could live life in reverse: born with lifelong wisdom, we would grow increasingly more youthful. But alas, we are destined to live with all the gains and losses of growing old. Abraham and Sarah are role models for older people. Their marriage had thrived through the crises of life: in midlife they took the risk to live their lives differently, they remained faithful through infertility, sexual jealousy, and family rivalry; they made sacrifices for each other and for their shared ideals, and most importantly, they left a legacy for future generations.

The span of Sarah's life confirms Sarah's great importance as Israel's first matriarch (verse 1). At her death, Abraham grieved for Sarah (verse 2). In the ancient world, mourning was never simply an interior emotion; it was also an external ritual. Abraham's mourning probably included wailing aloud, tearing his garment, cutting his beard, and putting on sackcloth for a set period of time. Though full of grief, Abraham had to see to the immediate practical need of finding a place for his wife's burial.

Because he was a resident alien, Abraham did not have an inherent right to buy land and he was at a significant disadvantage in seeking a burial plot for Sarah. The scene offers us a fascinating glimpse into the subtleties of Middle Eastern negotiations. Land was looked upon as an ancestral trust, and there was a deep-seated fear that selling land to a foreigner would upset the social balance of the community. For this reason, it seems like the whole town of Hebron is involved in Abraham's transaction. Through courteous give and take, bestowing polite titles and profound bows, a permanent burial cave is secured for the family of Abraham.

Abraham met the elders of Hebron at the city gates, where all official business was conducted. Identifying himself as a foreigner among the Hittites, he acknowledged that he was at their mercy. Because of Abraham's high status among the local townspeople, they first offered him the choicest burial place of the community (verse 6). But Abraham knew exactly which piece of property he wanted. It was the cave of Machpelah, located at the end of a field owned by Ephron son of Zohar (verses 8–9). Abraham wanted to own the property in perpetuity and was willing to do whatever was necessary to secure his ownership. To ensure that his descendants' claim to the property would not be contested in the future, Abraham insisted on paying a full price and on conducting the negotiations in full view of the citizens. When Ephron, with seeming nonchalance, offered to sell the entire field to Abraham for four hundred shekels of silver, Abraham immediately accepted his opening offer and weighed out the exact amount (verses 10–16). Abraham knew that, in the matter of his family's burial cave, a binding contract was more important than a good price.

Reflection and discussion

- What are the qualities that make Abraham and Sarah models for a healthy and lasting marriage? What of their example can I imitate?

- What was involved in the external rituals of grief and mourning in the time of the patriarchs and matriarchs?

- Could there be a link between monotheism (belief in one God) and monogamy (commitment to one spouse)? How does monotheism affect my commitments?

- Why are rituals of grief and mourning important today? How have such rituals help me heal after a loss?

- Have I thought about making arrangements for my funeral? How would I hope to be eulogized?

Prayer

God of the living and the dead, you want me to live my life in such a way that it becomes an example for the next generation. Keep me faithful and devoted to those I love so that my life might reflect the loyalty of your covenant with me.

LESSON 18  SESSION 4

Abraham breathed his last and died in a good old age, an old man and full of years, and was gathered to his people. His sons Isaac and Ishmael buried him in the cave of Machpelah. GENESIS 25:8–9

Burial of Sarah and Abraham

GENESIS 23:17–20 [17]*So the field of Ephron in Machpelah, which was to the east of Mamre, the field with the cave that was in it and all the trees that were in the field, throughout its whole area, passed* [18]*to Abraham as a possession in the presence of the Hittites, in the presence of all who went in at the gate of his city.* [19]*After this, Abraham buried Sarah his wife in the cave of the field of Machpelah facing Mamre (that is, Hebron) in the land of Canaan.* [20]*The field and the cave that is in it passed from the Hittites into Abraham's possession as a burying place.*

GENESIS 25:7–11 [7]*This is the length of Abraham's life, one hundred seventy-five years.* [8]*Abraham breathed his last and died in a good old age, an old man and full of years, and was gathered to his people.* [9]*His sons Isaac and Ishmael buried him in the cave of Machpelah, in the field of Ephron son of Zohar the Hittite, east of Mamre,* [10]*the field that Abraham purchased from the Hittites. There Abraham was buried, with his wife Sarah.* [11]*After the death of Abraham God blessed his son Isaac. And Isaac settled at Beer-lahai-roi.*

The cave of Machpelah in Hebron is the first piece of real estate in the promised land secured by the patriarch. Its purchase is confirmed in legal detail: identity of the transferor, location of the property, description of its contents, identity of the purchaser, and affirmation of official witnesses (23:17–18). Though it is a small piece of real estate, a single field with its trees and a cave, the importance of this sight is monumental for the future of Abraham's descendants.

By choosing to be buried in Canaan, rather than back in the land of their birth, Abraham and Sarah put down roots in the soil that God had promised to their descendants. The cave of Machpelah is the first foothold of a vast inheritance for future generations. According to Genesis, not only Abraham and Sarah are buried there but also Isaac and his wife Rebekah, and their son Jacob and his wife Leah. Throughout the biblical period, the cave was an important shrine and a symbol of Israelite unity.

Today the cave of Machpelah in Hebron is revered by Jews, Muslims, and Christians, since all the children of Abraham pay their respects to the great patriarchs and matriarchs. The Arab people identify the site as Haram el-Khalil, "the sacred precinct of the friend of God." The Jewish people consider it their most sacred monument after the Western Wall in Jerusalem. The surrounding wall of huge stones goes back to the time of Herod. Later in the Byzantine period, a church was built over the site, and with the Arab conquest in the seventh century, the church was converted into a mosque. Sadly, no place on earth, except for the temple mount in Jerusalem, has been the object of more violent struggle among Abraham's descendants.

After the burial of Sarah, Abraham lived another thirty-eight years. During those years, Abraham found a worthy bride for his son Isaac, as it was the custom of the time for parents to arrange their children's marriages (chapter 24). Abraham also married again, taking a wife named Keturah, with whom he had several more children who would also father nations (25:1–4). Though Isaac received his inheritance, Abraham provided for all of his children in his last years (25:5–6).

Abraham, like Sarah, lived a long and blessed life (25:7–8). After he exhaled the air of this world for the last time, both of his sons, Isaac and Ishmael, came together to bury their father, a task that transcended their rivalry (25:9). Both sons were loved by their father; both were promised abundant blessings; both would be fathers of nations. While the biblical story continues with Isaac and his family, Genesis does not fail to note the twelve sons of Ishmael (25:12–16), the descendants of whom were the Arab people (25:18). Many centuries later, some of the Arab people became the first followers of the Abrahamic faith that came to be called Islam. If there is to ever be peace between the offspring of Ishmael and Isaac, they must offer one another a reconciliation as profound as at the moment when the two brothers came together to bury their father Abraham.

Reflection and discussion

- In what way has my understanding of Abraham's spiritual paternity grown stronger after reflecting on these inspired texts?

- Why did Ishmael and Isaac come together to bury their father? What does this encounter teach me about forgiveness and reconciliation between individuals and among the peoples of the world?

- What parallels do I see between my journey of faith and that of Abraham and Sarah?

Prayer

God of our ancestors, from age to age you have gathered your people to yourself in death. May I remember those who have gone before me, my physical and spiritual ancestors, and trust that you will unite me with them, where we will praise you forever.

SUGGESTIONS FOR FACILITATORS, GROUP SESSION 4

1. Welcome group members and ask if anyone has any questions, announcements, or requests.

2. You may want to pray this prayer as a group:
   Everlasting God, you committed yourself to your people in the bond of the covenant, and you encourage us to make lasting commitments to others. Keep us faithful and devoted to those we love so that our lives might reflect the loyalty of your covenant. Give me the strength to always remain faithful to you and to trust your plan for my life. May we live our lives worthy of the great legacy we have been given by our ancestors and pass on our faith to the next generation.

3. Ask one of the following questions:
   - What is the most difficult part of this study for you?
   - What insights stand out to you from the lessons this week?

4. Discuss lessons 13 through 18. Choose one or more of the questions for reflection and discussion from each lesson to discuss as a group. You may want to ask group members which question was most challenging or helpful to them as you review each lesson.

5. Keep the discussion moving, but allow time for the questions that provoke the most discussion. Encourage the group members to use "I" language in their responses.

6. After talking over each lesson, instruct group members to complete lessons 19 through 24 on their own during the six days before the next group meeting. They should write out their own answers to the questions as preparation for next week's session.

7. Ask the group what encouragement they need for the coming week. Ask the members to pray for the needs of one another during the week.

8. Conclude by praying aloud together the prayer at the end of one of the lessons discussed. You may choose to conclude the prayer by asking members to pray aloud any requests they may have.

LESSON 19  SESSION 5

"I will bring you into the land that I swore to give to Abraham, Isaac, and Jacob; I will give it to you for a possession. I am the Lord." EXODUS 6:8

The Promise of God Made to Abraham

EXODUS 3:1–6, 13–16 *1 Moses was keeping the flock of his father-in-law Jethro,*
the priest of Midian; he led his flock beyond the wilderness, and came to Horeb,
the mountain of God. 2 There the angel of the Lord appeared to him in a flame of
fire out of a bush; he looked, and the bush was blazing, yet it was not consumed.
3 Then Moses said, "I must turn aside and look at this great sight, and see why the
bush is not burned up." 4 When the Lord saw that he had turned aside to see, God
called to him out of the bush, "Moses, Moses!" And he said, "Here I am." 5 Then he
said, "Come no closer! Remove the sandals from your feet, for the place on which
you are standing is holy ground." 6 He said further, "I am the God of your father,
the God of Abraham, the God of Isaac, and the God of Jacob." And Moses hid his
face, for he was afraid to look at God.

13 But Moses said to God, "If I come to the Israelites and say to them, 'The God
of your ancestors has sent me to you,' and they ask me, 'What is his name?' what
shall I say to them?" 14 God said to Moses, "I AM WHO I AM." He said further,
"Thus you shall say to the Israelites, 'I AM has sent me to you.'" 15 God also said to
Moses, "Thus you shall say to the Israelites, 'The Lord, the God of your ancestors,
the God of Abraham, the God of Isaac, and the God of Jacob, has sent me to you':

This is my name forever,
and this my title for all generations.
16Go and assemble the elders of Israel, and say to them, 'The Lord, the God of your
ancestors, the God of Abraham, of Isaac, and of Jacob, has appeared to me, saying:
I have given heed to you and to what has been done to you in Egypt.'"

EXODUS 6:2–9 *2God also spoke to Moses and said to him: "I am the Lord. 3I*
appeared to Abraham, Isaac, and Jacob as God Almighty, but by my name 'The
Lord' I did not make myself known to them. 4I also established my covenant with
them, to give them the land of Canaan, the land in which they resided as aliens.
5I have also heard the groaning of the Israelites whom the Egyptians are holding
as slaves, and I have remembered my covenant. 6Say therefore to the Israelites, 'I
am the Lord, and I will free you from the burdens of the Egyptians and deliver you
from slavery to them. I will redeem you with an outstretched arm and with mighty
acts of judgment. 7I will take you as my people, and I will be your God. You shall
know that I am the Lord your God, who has freed you from the burdens of the
Egyptians. 8I will bring you into the land that I swore to give to Abraham, Isaac,
and Jacob; I will give it to you for a possession. I am the Lord.'" 9Moses told this
to the Israelites; but they would not listen to Moses, because of their broken spirit
and their cruel slavery.

Many centuries after the life of Abraham, his descendants were living in the land of Egypt. The sons of Jacob, Abraham's great-grandsons, had gone to Egypt to escape from a famine in the land of Canaan. They continued to live there for many generations, and eventually they were made slaves of the Egyptians, being used as manual labor for the many building projects of the Pharaoh.

In offering Abraham a glimpse into the distant future, God had told him: "Know this for certain, that your offspring shall be aliens in a land that is not theirs, and shall be slaves there, and they shall be oppressed for four hundred years; but I will bring judgment on the nation that they serve, and afterward they shall come out with great possessions" (Gen 15:13–14). Having promised release from their bondage, God began to execute the exodus of Abraham's offspring from the slavery of Egypt by calling a man named Moses.

When God called to Moses from the midst of the blazing bush, he identified himself in a way that Moses would recognize: "I am the God of your father, the God of Abraham, the God of Isaac, and the God of Jacob (3:6, 15–16). This is the same God who had identified himself to Abraham as God Almighty (*El Shaddai*, in Hebrew) and entered into covenant with him (6:3; Gen 17:1–2). As Abraham had come to realize, this one God could not be localized in an idol, or controlled by ritual, or captured in a name. "I am who I am" (3:14) could only be known through his dynamic action in the lives of his people.

Just as God had rescued Sarah and Abraham long ago in Egypt by inflicting "plagues" on Pharaoh (Gen 12:17) and as God heard the cry of Hagar and Ishmael in their distress and came to their rescue (Gen 21:17), God has now heard the cry of the Hebrew people in Egypt and will come to release them from their bondage (6:5–6). God's covenant with Abraham is the all-important link with God from the past (6:3–4). God's promises given to Abraham long ago are now being actualized in God's liberating action on behalf of his struggling people.

The freedom that God wants for his people is not just a liberation from oppression; it is also the freedom to live in a land of blessing. The land that God had promised to Abraham and his posterity is the land to which God would bring Moses and his people. God said to Moses: "I will bring you into the land that I swore to give to Abraham, Isaac, and Jacob; I will give it to you for a possession" (6:8). The children of Abraham were coming back to the land of promise.

Reflection and discussion

- By what names does God identify himself to Moses? What do these names tell me about the nature of God?

- What is conveyed by God's identification of himself as "the God of Abraham"? What heritage and faith have I received from my ancestors?

- How reluctant am I to respond to God's call? What would it take to respond to him with an obedient heart?

- Take off your shoes and sit in the presence of the living God. How does this become "holy ground" for me?

Prayer

Lord God Almighty, you answer your people when they cry out to you, and you rescue the oppressed with your mighty hand. You are faithful through generation after generation. Help me trust in you.

He opened the rock, and water gushed out; it flowed through the desert like a river. For he remembered his holy promise, and Abraham, his servant.

PSALM 105:41–42

Song of Abraham's Offspring

PSALM 105:1–11

[1]*O give thanks to the Lord, call on his name,*
make known his deeds among the peoples.
[2]*Sing to him, sing praises to him;*
tell of all his wonderful works.
[3]*Glory in his holy name;*
let the hearts of those who seek the Lord rejoice.
[4]*Seek the Lord and his strength;*
seek his presence continually.
[5]*Remember the wonderful works he has done,*
his miracles, and the judgments he uttered,
[6]*O offspring of his servant Abraham,*
children of Jacob, his chosen ones.

[7]*He is the Lord our God;*
his judgments are in all the earth.
[8]*He is mindful of his covenant forever,*
of the word that he commanded, for a thousand generations,

[9]*the covenant that he made with Abraham,*
his sworn promise to Isaac,
[10]*which he confirmed to Jacob as a statute,*
to Israel as an everlasting covenant,
[11]*saying, "To you I will give the land of Canaan*
as your portion for an inheritance."

In the Psalms, the people of Israel express their faith through poetic song. Sung in the liturgies of Jerusalem's temple and in the communal celebrations of Israel's people, the Psalms convey the beliefs and emotions of the people of God. This psalm is a hymn of praise for God's trustworthiness and fidelity to the covenant.

Those addressed by the psalm are the "offspring of his servant Abraham" (verse 6). A series of imperatives calls the congregation to give thanks to the Lord, call on his name, make known his deeds, sing praises to him, tell his works, glory in his holy name, seek him, and remember his wonderful works (verses 1–5).

In forty-five verses the psalm recounts the primary historical deeds of God at work in the history of his people, from the covenant with Abraham through the exodus from Egypt and entry into the promised land. The entire series of wondrous events is the result of God's remembering the covenant with Abraham: "For he remembered his holy promise, and Abraham, his servant" (verse 42).

Abraham is called God's "servant" (verses 6, 42). In Israel's culture, a servant was a person who belonged to another and who lived in the context of that belonging. The servant's identity was determined by the one he served. In turn the servant was protected and supported by the person to whom the servant belonged. Thus the transfer was fairly easy from the concept of human servant to that of servant of God. In the Bible, those who give special service to God received the title of God's servant: first Abraham, then Moses, Joshua, prophets, kings, Israel, and the Messiah.

The primary theme of "covenant" (verses 8–11) stresses that the foundational events of salvation are God's initiative. He is the exclusive actor in the long list of wonderful works. God orchestrates everything for his people's benefit. The covenant is also called "the word," "sworn promise," and "statute." God's remembering the covenant has guided all God's actions in bringing his people into the land. The covenant is "everlasting." God will be mindful of his covenant "forever," "for a thousand generations." What God initiated in Abraham has only just begun.

Reflection and discussion

- What is the value of periodically "remembering" God's wonderful works? What are some of God's wonders I should remember?

- What does it mean to be a servant of God? What are its implications for my life?

- In what way are the events in my life's history the result of God's initiative?

Prayer

Lord God, in every age you remember the promises you made to Abraham. I thank you for the heritage of faith you have given me and for the blessings you have bestowed upon me. May I give you thanks, sing your praise, and make known your deeds.

Look to the rock from which you were hewn, and to the quarry from which you were dug. Look to Abraham your father and to Sarah who bore you. ISAIAH 51:1–2

The Rock and Quarry of Faith

ISAIAH 51:1–2

[1]*Listen to me, you that pursue righteousness,*
you that seek the Lord.
Look to the rock from which you were hewn,
and to the quarry from which you were dug.
[2]*Look to Abraham your father*
and to Sarah who bore you;
for he was but one when I called him,
but I blessed him and made him many.

SIRACH 44:19–21

[19]*Abraham was the great father of a multitude of nations,*
And no one has been found like him in glory.
[20]*He kept the law of the Most High,*
and entered into a covenant with him;
he certified the covenant with his flesh,
and when he was tested he proved faithful.
[21]*Therefore the Lord assured him with an oath*
that the nations would be blessed through his offspring;

that he would make him as numerous as the dust of the earth,
and exalt his offspring like the stars,
and give them an inheritance from sea to sea
and from the Euphrates to the ends of the earth.

This passage from the prophet Isaiah was written during the exile of the Jewish people in Babylon (sixth century B.C.) Though the exiles have remained faithful to God, they are discouraged and disheartened by their captivity and seeming powerlessness. They fear that, even if they are able to return to Judah, they will not be able to face the overwhelming task of restoring their homeland because they are so weak and few in numbers. Isaiah offers these exiles an encouraging message, calling them to look back to the example of their ancestors, Abraham and Sarah.

Though these exiles lived well over a thousand years after the lives of Abraham and Sarah, the prophet still holds up these ancestors as the inspiring model for their descendants to imitate. The metaphors of "rock" and "quarry" (Isa 51:1) refer to the solid conviction and foundational source of faith offered by Israel's patriarch and matriarch.

Though Abraham was elderly and childless when he was called, God "blessed him and made him many" (Isa 51:2). Based on God's assurances to Abraham and Sarah, the exiles can be confident that God will bless them with strength and abundance as they prepare to make the same journey made by their ancestors, returning to their home in the promised land. The promises God made to Abraham and Sarah will continue to be fulfilled in every age.

The book of Sirach was written by a Jewish teacher in Jerusalem (second century B.C.) who wanted to instill within his young students a loving respect for the traditions of their ancestors. Sirach wanted to help his students find a balance between living in the contemporary world and respecting the faith of their ancestors. The final chapters of his work consist of a poetic hymn of praise to the heroes of Israel's past, seeking to motivate his young hearers to similar loyalty.

Sirach refers to Abraham as "the great father of a multitude of nations" (Sir 44:19). He then lists four of Abraham's outstanding merits: he kept God's law, he made a covenant with God, he certified the covenant through circumcision, and he proved faithful when he was tested (Sir 44:20). In response, God assured Abraham of three promises: the nations would be blessed through his offspring, his progeny would be as numerous as the dust of the earth and as exalted as the stars, and his posterity would receive a vast inheritance (Sir 44:21). "Sea to sea" and "to the ends of the earth" express an idealistic expanse and the universal breadth of Abraham's blessings.

Reflection and discussion

- In what areas of my life do I feel discouraged and powerless? What word of hope do these Scriptures offer to me?

- Why are the terms "rock" and "quarry" effective metaphors for describing the role of our biblical ancestors?

- In what way could Abraham and Sarah be models and inspirations for young people today? What qualities do they inspire in the young?

Prayer

Most High God, you called our ancestors to a committed life in covenant with you. Help me to learn from their example and be inspired by their heroism so that I may leave a legacy to the generations after me.

The scripture, foreseeing that God would justify the Gentiles by faith, declared the gospel beforehand to Abraham, saying, "All the Gentiles shall be blessed in you." For this reason, those who believe are blessed with Abraham who believed. GALATIANS 3:8

Descendants of Abraham through Faith

GALATIANS 3:6–9, 15–18 *[6]Just as Abraham "believed God, and it was reck-*
oned to him as righteousness," [7]so, you see, those who believe are the descendants
of Abraham. [8]And the scripture, foreseeing that God would justify the Gentiles by
faith, declared the gospel beforehand to Abraham, saying, "All the Gentiles shall
be blessed in you." [9]For this reason, those who believe are blessed with Abraham
who believed.

[15]Brothers and sisters, I give an example from daily life: once a person's will
has been ratified, no one adds to it or annuls it. [16]Now the promises were made to
Abraham and to his offspring; it does not say, "And to offsprings," as of many; but
it says, "And to your offspring," that is, to one person, who is Christ. [17]My point is
this: the law, which came four hundred thirty years later, does not annul a cove-
nant previously ratified by God, so as to nullify the promise. [18]For if the inheritance
comes from the law, it no longer comes from the promise; but God granted it to
Abraham through the promise.

Jesus was a Jew, a "son of Abraham," as the opening verse of the New Testament declares (Matt 1:1). All the major figures in the life of Jesus and the early church were from the people of Israel, and the church began as a sect of Judaism. Paul himself was proud of his Jewish heritage, as he frequently testified in his letters: "I myself am an Israelite, a descendant of Abraham" (Rom 11:1). When Paul began his missionary travels, he would always preach first in the synagogue of each town he visited. Though Jesus had certainly opened a new era in the history of God's relationship with his chosen people, for Paul that newness was in continuity with God's actions in Israel's history.

Paul's Letter to the Galatians focuses on the issues that arose as non-Jews (Gentiles) began to accept the good news of Jesus Christ. Paul was convinced that the gospel by its very nature was directed to Gentiles as well as to Jews, but he was equally convinced that Jesus was the fulfillment of Jewish expectations rooted in the promises contained in the ancient Scriptures. The fundamental questions, then, are the following: In light of the coming of Christ, who makes up the people of God? What is the distinguishing characteristic of God's people? Who, in fact, are "descendants of Abraham"?

Paul responds to these questions by quoting from the accounts of Abraham in Genesis. First, he quotes Genesis 15:6 which states: Abraham "believed the Lord; and the Lord reckoned it to him as righteousness." Paul explains that Abraham's belief in God was the characteristic that brought about his right relationship with God. Therefore, Abraham's true descendants must be those who "believe," those who relate to God through faith (verses 6–7). This means that, for Paul, the distinctive characteristic of being the people of God is faith, not biological descent or following the law given to Moses.

Paul's second quote is from Genesis 12:3 which states: In Abraham, "all the families of the earth shall be blessed." Paul acclaims this verse as a foreshadowing of the good news, "the gospel beforehand" (verse 8). This message of good news implies that at some future time all the nations (Gentiles as well as Jews) will be blessed as heirs of Abraham. For Paul, Christ is the fulfillment of this hope. His salvation is offered to all people who accept God's grace in faith. The movement of the gospel of Jesus Christ outward to the Gentiles is not just Paul's way of extending the mission; it was God's plan since the call of Abraham.

The truest "offspring" of Abraham is Christ (verse 16). His life has redefined the people of God and opened the door to the whole world. Paul points out that the "promise" given to Abraham preceded the "law" given to Moses by four hundred and thirty years (verses 17–18). Since the covenant with Moses cannot negate the covenant with Abraham, entry into the people of God is through believing in the promise, not just obeying the law. The sole criteria for sharing in God's blessings is faith in Christ, not following the prescripts of the law.

Reflection and discussion

- Why does Paul describe Genesis 12:3 as "the gospel beforehand"? In what way is this verse a foreshadowing of the good news of Christ during the time of Abraham?

- In what way does Paul broaden the Jewish understanding of "descendants of Abraham" (verse 7)? In what way am I a descendant of Abraham?

- What aspects of the gospel of Jesus Christ convince me that it is destined for all people, not just for its first Jewish followers?

Prayer

Lord God, your promises extend from Abraham to all the people of the world. Help me to receive your promises with trusting confidence so that I may truly be a descendant of Abraham and a member of your people.

What does the scripture say? "Abraham believed God, and it was reckoned to him as righteousness." ROMANS 4:3

Our Example of Faith

ROMANS 4:1–12 1 *What then are we to say was gained by Abraham, our ancestor*
according to the flesh? 2 *For if Abraham was justified by works, he has something*
to boast about, but not before God. 3 *For what does the scripture say? "Abraham*
believed God, and it was reckoned to him as righteousness." 4 *Now to one who*
works, wages are not reckoned as a gift but as something due. 5 *But to one who*
without works trusts him who justifies the ungodly, such faith is reckoned as righ-
teousness. 6 *So also David speaks of the blessedness of those to whom God reckons*
righteousness apart from works:

7 *"Blessed are those whose iniquities are forgiven,*
and whose sins are covered;
8 *blessed is the one against whom the Lord will not reckon sin."*

9 *Is this blessedness, then, pronounced only on the circumcised, or also on the uncir-*
cumcised? We say, "Faith was reckoned to Abraham as righteousness." 10 *How then*
was it reckoned to him? Was it before or after he had been circumcised? It was not
after, but before he was circumcised. 11 *He received the sign of circumcision as a seal*
of the righteousness that he had by faith while he was still uncircumcised. The pur-
pose was to make him the ancestor of all who believe without being circumcised
and who thus have righteousness reckoned to them, 12 *and likewise the ancestor of*
the circumcised who are not only circumcised but who also follow the example of
the faith that our ancestor Abraham had before he was circumcised.

The figure of Abraham is more prominent in Paul's writings than any other individual except for Jesus. Here Paul invokes Abraham as his exemplar to verify the proposal he set forth in Romans 3:28: "For we hold that a person is justified by faith apart from works prescribed by the law." In order to demonstrate this truth, Paul refers to the life of Abraham as recorded in Genesis. Abraham continually believed in God's promises of a son and the blessings that would ensue despite overwhelming evidence to the contrary and seemingly insurmountable obstacles: Sarah's barrenness, his own old age, the rejection of Ishmael, and decades of waiting. Abraham's own resources were exhausted; there was nothing Abraham himself could do. The only choice was humble submission and confident trust. Thus, "Abraham believed God" (verse 3), personally and completely.

Abraham's achievements were utterly extraordinary. He left the civilization of Ur to travel to an unknown land, he carved out a life for Sarah and himself in the nomadic wilderness of Canaan, he fought battles with desert kings, he interceded for Sodom before God, and he demonstrated a willingness to sacrifice even his beloved son. If anyone had a reason to boast, it would be Abraham (verse 2). But despite the praiseworthiness of these deeds, they were of no consequence in realizing God's promises. Abraham simply trusted in the credibility of God. He was not justified by his works, but by his faith.

God's promises to Abraham were not a reward for Abraham's obedience and good performance, for God called Abraham and promised him blessings and progeny before he had responded in obedience (Gen 12:1–3). It was Abraham's faith in God that justified him: "Abraham believed God, and it was reckoned to him as righteousness" (verse 3). God regarded Abraham as righteous (Gen 15:6) before Abraham had been either tested (Gen 22) or circumcised (Gen 17). His blessings were not given by God as a reward for something good he had done, like wages given to a worker (verse 4). Righteousness was not Abraham's due; it was God's gift, the act of God's gracious will.

Abraham is the bearer of God's promised blessings to all people. Because he is our father in faith, when we share in his faith we become his descendants. For Paul and other Jews, Abraham is their "ancestor according to the flesh" (verse 1). But for everyone else, Abraham is the "ancestor of all who believe" (verse 11). We become descendants of Abraham by sharing his faithful trust, not his genes.

Paul's Jewish contemporaries believed that God justifies those within the covenant, while the "ungodly" stand outside the covenant. But Paul taught that God justifies the "ungodly" (verse 5) through their faith and bestows blessings on both the circumcised and the uncircumcised (verses 9–12). If God justified Abraham before he was circumcised, then he was not a Jew at the time of his justification. Abraham was an uncircumcised Gentile when he was reckoned righteous by God. Thus Abraham was the father of Gentile believers before he was the father of Jewish believers. His becoming forefather of the Jewish people followed his fatherhood of all believers.

For Paul and the early Christian church, this meant that both Gentile and Jewish followers of Jesus could appeal to Abraham as father. Both groups are included within Abraham's fatherhood of faith, and neither is pitted against the other. There is not one way to salvation for Jews and another for Gentiles. Through Abraham we know that trusting faith in God is not a new means to salvation, supplanting the keeping of the law, but rather the oldest and truest means.

Reflection and discussion

- What parts of Abraham's life are most extraordinary and praiseworthy to me? Why does Abraham not boast in his accomplishments?

- How is Abraham the father not only of Jews but of all believers?

- Does it matter to me whether a right relationship with God is a gift to be received or a reward to be earned? What difference does it make to me practically and emotionally?

- What are the global implications of the fact that Abraham is the father of all believers?

- How do Paul's words inspire me with a desire to evangelize and share my faith with those around me?

Prayer

God of our ancestors, through the cross of Jesus Christ you extended the blessings promised to Abraham to the whole world. Help me realize that I cannot earn your salvation but that I can only accept the gift of your saving grace through a living faith in Christ.

Hoping against hope, he believed that he would become "the father of many nations," according to what was said, "So numerous shall your descendants be." ROMANS 4:18

God's Promises Inherited through Faith

ROMANS 4:13–25 [13]*For the promise that he would inherit the world did not come to Abraham or to his descendants through the law but through the righteousness of faith.* [14]*If it is the adherents of the law who are to be the heirs, faith is null and the promise is void.* [15]*For the law brings wrath; but where there is no law, neither is there violation.*

[16]*For this reason it depends on faith, in order that the promise may rest on grace and be guaranteed to all his descendants, not only to the adherents of the law but also to those who share the faith of Abraham (for he is the father of all of us,* [17]*as it is written, "I have made you the father of many nations") —in the presence of the God in whom he believed, who gives life to the dead and calls into existence the things that do not exist.* [18]*Hoping against hope, he believed that he would become "the father of many nations," according to what was said, "So numerous shall your descendants be."* [19]*He did not weaken in faith when he considered his own body, which was already as good as dead (for he was about a hundred years old), or when he considered the barrenness of Sarah's womb.* [20]*No distrust made him waver concerning the promise of God, but he grew strong in his faith as he gave glory to God,* [21]*being fully convinced that God was able to do what he had promised.* [22]*Therefore his faith "was reckoned to him as righteousness."*

[23]Now the words, "it was reckoned to him," were written not for his sake alone,
[24]but for ours also. It will be reckoned to us who believe in him who raised Jesus our
Lord from the dead, [25]who was handed over to death for our trespasses and was
raised for our justification.

Paul refers to God's promise that Abraham would "inherit the world" (verse 13). That promise, given to Abraham nearly two millennia before Paul, would not remain the possession of only one segment of humanity. Like yeast in the dough, Abraham's descendants would grow to permeate the whole world. His offspring would surpass the bounds of Israel and include the Gentiles so that God's salvation would be offered to everyone. His heirs would be all people who walk by faith. He is the "father of many nations"; he is the "father of us all" (verses 16–18).

The God in whom Abraham believed is the God "who gives life to the dead and calls into existence the things that do not exist" (verse 17). Abraham experienced these manifestations of the God of life. The bodies of Abraham and Sarah were dead to the possibility of producing an heir. At the moment when their beloved son was doomed to die in sacrifice, God restored him to life. The creating and redeeming God of Abraham brought an inheritance into being in a way that seemed totally impossible.

The only response to such a God is faith. Trying to earn the favor of such a God or merit his blessings would be foolish. But faith in the God of the impossible brings hope for the future. God transformed the obstacles Abraham encountered into possibilities for something beyond his dreams. Abraham's faith was not an easy choice; it was a constant struggle. He questioned God, doubted God, pleaded with God. And through this struggle his faith became stronger. For Abraham, the final word was always God's promises (verses 20–21).

This same God of the impossible was also Paul's God. And Paul convinces us through his writing that this same creating and redeeming God is our God too. The God of Abraham is the God "who raised Jesus our Lord from the dead" (verse 24). The faith of Abraham is a model for all believers—Jews and Gentiles. It is the same faith in the same God who brings the dead to life.

Abraham is the key to understanding the meaning of God's grace and our appropriate response in faith. God's call and promise to Abraham were independent of Abraham's merit or achievement. Justification by grace through faith, creation from nothing, and resurrection from the dead are all affirmations about the same reality. They bear witness to the power of God to evoke new life in situations where there is nothing on which to base hope. The God of the impossible still brings laughter into the world.

Reflection and discussion

- God transformed the obstacles Abraham encountered into possibilities for something beyond his dreams. How has God transformed the obstacles of my life into something I had never imagined?

- In what ways do justification through faith, creation from nothing, and resurrection from the dead characterize the work of the God of the impossible (verse 17)? How does God manifest himself to me as the God of the impossible?

- Often it is easier to be paid for something we have earned rather than accept the generosity of God. Why is faith such a struggle for me?

Prayer

Creating and Redeeming God, you create out of nothing and raise the dead to life. I thank you for offering me the gift of salvation, not through my own merits, but through Christ, "who was handed over to death for our trespasses and was raised for our justification."

SUGGESTIONS FOR FACILITATORS, GROUP SESSION 5

1. Welcome group members and ask if anyone has any questions, announcements, or requests.

2. You may want to pray this prayer as a group:
   Most High God, you are faithful through generation after generation, remembering the promises you made to Abraham and Sarah. As the God of our ancestors, you answer your people when they cry out to you, and you rescue the oppressed with your mighty hand. Through the saving cross of Jesus, your promised blessings extend to the whole world. Help me to accept the gift of your redeeming grace through a living relationship with your Son. I thank you for the heritage of faith you have given me as I trust in you, sing your praise, and make known your deeds.

3. Ask one or both of the following questions:
   - What most intrigued you from this week's study?
   - What makes you want to know and understand more of God's word?

4. Discuss lessons 19 through 24. Choose one or more of the questions for reflection and discussion from each lesson to talk over as a group.

5. Ask the group members to name one thing they have most appreciated about the way the group has worked during this Bible study. Ask group members to discuss any changes they might suggest in the way the group works in future studies.

6. Invite group members to complete lessons 25 through 30 on their own during the six days before the next meeting. They should write out their own answers to the questions as preparation for next week's session.

7. Ask group members how their study of Abraham and Sarah is helping them appreciate the legacy of faith they have received.

8. Conclude by praying aloud together the prayer at the end of one of the lessons discussed. You may want to conclude the prayer by asking members to voice prayers of thanksgiving.

LESSON 25  SESSION 6

Thus he has shown the mercy promised to our ancestors, and has remembered his holy covenant, the oath that he swore to our ancestor Abraham. LUKE 1:72–73

Remembering the Covenant of Old

LUKE 1:57–75 *57 Now the time came for Elizabeth to give birth, and she bore a son. 58 Her neighbors and relatives heard that the Lord had shown his great mercy to her, and they rejoiced with her.*

59 On the eighth day they came to circumcise the child, and they were going to name him Zechariah after his father. 60 But his mother said, "No; he is to be called John." 61 They said to her, "None of your relatives has this name." 62 Then they began motioning to his father to find out what name he wanted to give him. 63 He asked for a writing tablet and wrote, "His name is John." And all of them were amazed. 64 Immediately his mouth was opened and his tongue freed, and he began to speak, praising God. 65 Fear came over all their neighbors, and all these things were talked about throughout the entire hill country of Judea. 66 All who heard them pondered them and said, "What then will this child become?" For, indeed, the hand of the Lord was with him.

67 Then his father Zechariah was filled with the Holy Spirit and spoke this prophecy:

68 "Blessed be the Lord God of Israel,
for he has looked favorably on his people and redeemed them.
69 He has raised up a mighty savior for us
in the house of his servant David,

70as he spoke through the mouth of his holy prophets from of old,
71that we would be saved from our enemies and from the hand of all who hate us.
72Thus he has shown the mercy promised to our ancestors,
and has remembered his holy covenant,
73the oath that he swore to our ancestor Abraham,
to grant us 74that we, being rescued from the hands of our enemies,
might serve him without fear, 75in holiness and righteousness
before him all our days.

Luke's gospel proclaims that God has remembered his covenant and kept the promises he made long ago with Abraham. In Jesus, a new period of God's saving plan has begun. This new age of salvation in Jesus Christ is the fulfillment of what God had in mind from ages past, the completion of a pattern that God had begun in Abraham almost two thousand years before. What had begun with one person in Abraham was destined to be experienced by all people as the gospel spreads to the east, west, north, and south and breaks down barriers that divide people—Jew and Gentile, rich and poor, man and woman, mighty and humble.

The canticle of Zechariah, the father of John the Baptist, is a programmatic prophecy (verses 67–75). It is a summary of what God is about to do through the coming of Jesus into the world, and it guides the readers' understanding through the narrative that follows. The prophecy draws heavily from Old Testament texts and prophetic allusions to indicate the continuity of God's plan throughout the generations.

It is significant that the covenant of God with Abraham, "the oath that he swore to our ancestor Abraham" (verse 73), is more fundamental than the covenant with Moses. For Luke, the first Christians are the "descendants of Abraham," through whom the blessings are delivered. Luke makes this clear in his writings in Acts by quoting from the speech of Peter to the believers in Jerusalem: "You are the descendants of the prophets and of the covenant that God gave to your ancestors, saying to Abraham, 'And in your descendants all the families of the earth shall be blessed'" (Acts 3:25).

The occasion of Zechariah's canticle is the circumcision of his son John on the eighth day after his birth (verse 59). How fitting for Zechariah to celebrate "the oath that [God] swore to our ancestor Abraham" at that event! God had first revealed the sign of circumcision to Abraham, who performed the ritual on his sons. The infant John, who would be the prophet called to announce the arrival of the Messiah, was initiated into the ancient faith of Israel and would live his whole life in dedication to that covenant.

The elderly Zechariah and Elizabeth, like their ancestors Abraham and Sarah from so long before, had been living their later life in hopelessness because of their childless state. Yet they were miraculously blessed by God with a child. Again "the Lord God of Israel" has "looked favorably on his people" (verse 68). What God had done at the beginning of salvation history in Abraham and Sarah was now unfolding again as a new age began.

The other programmatic prophecy of Luke's first chapter is Mary's canticle. The gospel of Luke is about how God reverses destinies: bringing down the powerful and lifting the lowly, filling the hungry with blessings and sending the rich away empty. All of this is "according to the promises he made to our ancestors, to Abraham and to his descendants forever" (1:51–55).

Reflection and discussion

- How does the canticle of Zechariah indicate the continuity of God's saving plan, from Abraham and Sarah to the coming of Christ?

- In what ways is the first couple of salvation history (Abraham and Sarah) like the first couple of the New Testament (Zechariah and Elizabeth)?

- What is God demonstrating in bringing fertility and birth to elderly and barren couples? In what ways am I barren and in need of new birth?

- How does Luke indicate that the first Christians are the descendants of Abraham and heirs of God's covenant with Abraham? In what way am I included in Luke's understanding of God's plan?

- Zechariah's life was transformed through the word of God delivered to him. In what way am I being formed and changed through this gospel text?

Prayer

Blessed are you, Lord God of Israel. You have looked with favor on your people and proven yourself faithful to your covenant of old. You raised up a mighty Savior for us in your Son, Jesus. May I serve you in holiness and righteousness all my days.

LESSON 26  SESSION 6

The poor man died and was carried away by the angels to be with Abraham. The rich man also died and was buried. In Hades, where he was being tormented, he looked up and saw Abraham far away with Lazarus by his side. LUKE 16:22–23

Father Abraham, Have Mercy on Me

LUKE 16:19–31 19*“There was a rich man who was dressed in purple and fine linen
and who feasted sumptuously every day.* 20*And at his gate lay a poor man named
Lazarus, covered with sores,* 21*who longed to satisfy his hunger with what fell from
the rich man’s table; even the dogs would come and lick his sores.* 22*The poor man
died and was carried away by the angels to be with Abraham. The rich man also
died and was buried.* 23*In Hades, where he was being tormented, he looked up and
saw Abraham far away with Lazarus by his side.* 24*He called out, ‘Father Abraham,
have mercy on me, and send Lazarus to dip the tip of his finger in water and cool my
tongue; for I am in agony in these flames.’* 25*But Abraham said, ‘Child, remember
that during your lifetime you received your good things, and Lazarus in like manner
evil things; but now he is comforted here, and you are in agony.* 26*Besides all this,
between you and us a great chasm has been fixed, so that those who might want to
pass from here to you cannot do so, and no one can cross from there to us.’* 27*He said,
‘Then, father, I beg you to send him to my father’s house—* 28*for I have five brothers—that he may warn them, so that they will not also come into this place of torment.’* 29*Abraham replied, ‘They have Moses and the prophets; they should listen to
them.’* 30*He said, ‘No, father Abraham; but if someone goes to them from the dead,
they will repent.’* 31*He said to him, ‘If they do not listen to Moses and the prophets,
neither will they be convinced even if someone rises from the dead.’”*

The narratives of Abraham in Genesis contain dramatic accounts of how God reverses the human condition: blessing the barren with fertility, bringing an heir to the childless, blessing the outcaste slave in the wilderness, rescuing from imminent death. The gospel of Luke, too, is filled with dramatic reversals: bringing down the powerful, lifting up the lowly, filling the hungry with blessings, sending the rich away empty.

This parable of Jesus continues this theme of reversals. The situations of the rich man and Lazarus could not be more starkly contrasted. The rich man dressed in the finest clothing and feasted sumptuously, not just on special occasions, but "every day" (verse 19). The poor man was covered with ulcerated sores and lay among the dogs. Starving, he longed to eat the scraps that fell from the table of the rich man (verses 20–21). Lazarus lay at the gate of the rich man's home, so evidently the rich man passed him by each day without notice or concern.

Both men died: the poor man obviously from starvation and disease, the rich man probably from conditions that afflict those who feast habitually on rich foods and strong drink. But in the next life their conditions are dramatically reversed. The rich man ends in torment, and the poor man rests at the side of Abraham (verses 22–23). The one who failed to show mercy in his earthly life now begs for mercy from "Father Abraham" (verse 24). Not only are their roles reversed, but they are intensified. Abraham's reply sums up the dramatic turnaround: the one who received good things during his lifetime is in "agony" in the afterlife, while the one who received evil things on earth is "comforted" in Abraham's embrace (verse 25). The rich man's agony far exceeds the misery that poor Lazarus had ever experienced in life, while the bliss of Lazarus far exceeds the pleasure the rich man had ever experienced.

According to Jewish midrash, Abraham will sit at the entrance to hell to make sure that no circumcised Israelite is cast in. He has the authority to rescue them and receive them into heaven. With these legends in mind, the rich man believed that Abraham would give him comfort by sending Lazarus either to bring him a drop of cool water or warn his five brothers to repent (verses 24, 27–28). But, as John the Baptist has already indicated, it is not enough to claim "we have Abraham as our ancestor." Rather, the children of Abraham must "bear fruits worthy of repentance" (Luke 3:8).

The rich man's neglect of the poor man at his gate was a clear rejection of "Moses and the prophets" (verse 29). The law of Moses demanded: "If there is among you anyone in need,...do not be hard-hearted or tight-fisted toward your needy neighbor" (Deut 15:7). Likewise, the prophets do not relent: "Share your bread with the hungry, and bring the homeless person into your house" (Isa 58:7). Abraham declared, finally, that if the rich man's brothers do not listen to Moses and the prophets, they will not be convinced "even if someone rises from the dead" (verse 31). Those who refuse to obey the clear words of the Scriptures will also reject the message of the risen Christ.

Reflection and discussion

- Since the rich man and his brothers have the clear teachings of the Scriptures, what is their problem? When do I have similar problems in grasping the meaning of Scripture?

- What words of this parable have the most impact on me? What parts of the parable make me uncomfortable?

- The biblical story, from beginning to end, seems to be a series of reversals. How does this reality help me understand the meaning of the Christian life?

Prayer

God of Abraham and Father of Jesus, you are the God of the living and the dead. May I live my life in such a way as to give glory to you. Give me a compassionate heart so that I will notice and heed the needs of those around me.

LESSON 27  SESSION 6

They answered him, "Abraham is our father." Jesus said to them, "If you were Abraham's children, you would be doing what Abraham did." JOHN 8:39

Doing What Abraham Did

JOHN 8:31–42 *31 Then Jesus said to the Jews who had believed in him, "If you continue in my word, you are truly my disciples; 32 and you will know the truth, and the truth will make you free." 33 They answered him, "We are descendants of Abraham and have never been slaves to anyone. What do you mean by saying, 'You will be made free'?"*

34 Jesus answered them, "Very truly, I tell you, everyone who commits sin is a slave to sin. 35 The slave does not have a permanent place in the household; the son has a place there forever. 36 So if the Son makes you free, you will be free indeed. 37 I know that you are descendants of Abraham; yet you look for an opportunity to kill me, because there is no place in you for my word. 38 I declare what I have seen in the Father's presence; as for you, you should do what you have heard from the Father."

39 They answered him, "Abraham is our father." Jesus said to them, "If you were Abraham's children, you would be doing what Abraham did, 40 but now you are trying to kill me, a man who has told you the truth that I heard from God. This is not what Abraham did. 41 You are indeed doing what your father does." They said to him, "We are not illegitimate children; we have one father, God himself." 42 Jesus said to them, "If God were your Father, you would love me, for I came from God and now I am here. I did not come on my own, but he sent me.

The dialogue between Jesus and those Jews who have taken a hostile position toward him revolves around the question of paternity: Who is our Father? To be a child of a father means listening to the word of that father and doing what he does. What does it mean to be a child of Abraham? Is it a matter of physical descent, or something more? If God is our Father, what does that imply? Surely children of the same father would love one another.

Jesus proclaimed that by believing in his word, his disciples would know the truth, and that truth would set them free (verses 31–32). His antagonists, however, proclaimed that they are descendants of Abraham, and as Abraham's posterity they have always been spiritually free and never slaves (verse 33). Jesus responded that it is sin that makes us slaves and that prevents us from having a secure place in God's household (verses 34–35). To have a permanent place in the household, we must be children of God, a status that we receive through believing the word of Jesus and coming to know the truth. The freedom that results from this personal acceptance of the saving word of Jesus is a deep confidence and interior freedom that results from an intimate relationship with God (verse 36).

Resisting the invitation of Jesus, his listeners claim: "Abraham is our father" (verse 39). Jesus acknowledges that they are physical descendants of Abraham, just as he himself is (verse 37). But bloodline does not determine genuine sonship and freedom. True children do what their father does. If they were true children of Abraham they "would be doing what Abraham did." Unlike Abraham, they have not opened their lives to the transforming power of God's word. Abraham was a man of faith, from his response to God's call to leave his homeland to his willingness to offer his son to God. When God sent the divine messengers to Abraham (Gen 18), the faithful patriarch welcomed them. But the opponents of Jesus have rejected the word of God made known in Jesus, the heavenly messenger, and are trying to kill him (verse 40).

Jesus teaches that there is no contradiction between being a child of Abraham and a child of God. All who listen to God like Abraham and respond in action to God's word are truly Abraham's descendants. And all these children of Abraham are free children of God, living permanently in the household of God. Indeed, Israel is described in the Scriptures as God's firstborn son (Exod 4:22). Since Jesus is from God and beloved of God, surely all those who have God as their Father should accept the one sent from God. Children of the same Father should love one another (verses 41–42).

Reflection and discussion

- Who are the true descendants of Abraham? What is required to be identified as a child of Abraham?

- Jesus taught: "You will know the truth, and the truth will make you free" (verse 32). What is the practical meaning of this verse in my own life?

- In what ways has my faith been communicated to me through my family tree? Why is receiving faith from my ancestors not enough to be a child of my Father's household?

Prayer

Lord Jesus, open my ears to hear your word and open my heart to accept it. Remove from my life all that would distort your word so that I can experience the freedom that comes from living in your truth.

The Jews said to Jesus, "You are not yet fifty years old, and have you seen Abraham?" Jesus said to them, "Very truly, I tell you, before Abraham was, I am." JOHN 8:57–58

Greater than Our Father Abraham

JOHN 8:48–59 48 *The Jews answered him, "Are we not right in saying that you are*
a Samaritan and have a demon?" 49 *Jesus answered, "I do not have a demon; but*
I honor my Father, and you dishonor me. 50 *Yet I do not seek my own glory; there*
is one who seeks it and he is the judge. 51 *Very truly, I tell you, whoever keeps my*
word will never see death." 52 *The Jews said to him, "Now we know that you have*
a demon. Abraham died, and so did the prophets; yet you say, 'Whoever keeps
my word will never taste death.' 53 *Are you greater than our father Abraham, who*
died? The prophets also died. Who do you claim to be?" 54 *Jesus answered, "If I glo-*
rify myself, my glory is nothing. It is my Father who glorifies me, he of whom you
say, 'He is our God,' 55 *though you do not know him. But I know him; if I would*
say that I do not know him, I would be a liar like you. But I do know him and I
keep his word. 56 *Your ancestor Abraham rejoiced that he would see my day; he*
saw it and was glad." 57 *Then the Jews said to him, "You are not yet fifty years old,*
and have you seen Abraham?" 58 *Jesus said to them, "Very truly, I tell you, before*
Abraham was, I am." 59 *So they picked up stones to throw at him, but Jesus hid*
himself and went out of the temple.

Having proclaimed that continuing in his word brings knowledge of the truth and genuine freedom (8:31–32), Jesus proclaims another astonishing promise: "Whoever keeps my word will never see death" (verse 51). Abiding in the word of Jesus, living out its demands, taking it to heart, leads to a life that lasts forever.

Again the words of Jesus are rejected by his opponents with an appeal to Abraham (verses 52–53). Surely, they say, Jesus could not be greater than their father Abraham. Abraham and all the prophets after him died; how can Jesus offer eternal life?

Jesus counters his opponents' appeal to Abraham with an appeal to God himself, the supreme Life-giver (verses 54–55). Though the Jews who have taken a hostile position toward Jesus claim they are children of Abraham, Jesus says that Abraham accepted God's designs while they do not. Abraham rejoiced that he was to see the day of Jesus (verse 56), while they do not. Abraham looked forward to the accomplishments of God in the new age. He believed God's promise that through his offspring blessings would eventually come to the whole world (Gen 12:3). From this biblical promise came a Jewish rabbinical tradition that Abraham had been given a revelation of the secrets of the age to come, especially the age of the Messiah. For this reason, Jesus claimed that Abraham foresaw the time of Jesus and was glad.

Asked how Jesus could possibly have seen Abraham since Jesus lived almost two millennia after Abraham's lifetime, Jesus responded with the most amazing claim yet: "Very truly, I tell you, before Abraham was, I am" (verse 58). The Son of God, the Word of God, was already in existence from the beginning. The opening words of John's gospel, evoking the opening words of Genesis, had proclaimed, "In the beginning was the Word" (John 1:1). Existing from eternity, Jesus transcended time. He speaks with the voice of the God of Abraham, Isaac, and Jacob, the God of the living. He is the source of life and hope even for Abraham and all the prophets. This claim to divinity was too much for the crowd who rejected his message, and they took up stones to cast at this blasphemer.

For reflection

- How does Jesus fulfill God's promises to Abraham? How does he fulfill God's promises to me?

- What are the deepest hopes of all people? What assures me that I can entrust my future to Jesus?

- Of the three solemn claims made by Jesus in this encounter (verses 32, 51, 58), which strikes me the most strongly and offers me the most hope?

Prayer

Divine Lord, you are the hope of Israel and of all the nations of the earth. Let your word penetrate my heart, make me secure in your promises, and lead me to eternal life.

LESSON 29  SESSION 6

"And so Abraham became the father of Isaac and circumcised him on the eighth day; and Isaac became the father of Jacob, and Jacob of the twelve patriarchs." ACTS 7:8

The Line of Abraham's Descendants

ACTS 7:1–8 [1]*Then the high priest asked him, "Are these things so?"* [2]*And Stephen*
replied: "Brothers and fathers, listen to me. The God of glory appeared to our ancestor
Abraham when he was in Mesopotamia, before he lived in Haran, [3]*and said to him,*
'Leave your country and your relatives and go to the land that I will show you.' [4]*Then*
he left the country of the Chaldeans and settled in Haran. After his father died, God
had him move from there to this country in which you are now living. [5]*He did not give*
him any of it as a heritage, not even a foot's length, but promised to give it to him as his
possession and to his descendants after him, even though he had no child. [6]*And God*
spoke in these terms, that his descendants would be resident aliens in a country belong-
ing to others, who would enslave them and mistreat them during four hundred years.
[7]*'But I will judge the nation that they serve,' said God, 'and after that they shall come*
out and worship me in this place.' [8]*Then he gave him the covenant of circumcision.*
And so Abraham became the father of Isaac and circumcised him on the eighth day;
and Isaac became the father of Jacob, and Jacob of the twelve patriarchs."

The arrest, speech, and martyrdom of Stephen (Acts 6–7) is a turning point in the early days of the church in Jerusalem, as narrated in the Acts of the Apostles. His death and the ensuing persecution launched the church's expansion to the surrounding regions and eventually into the whole world (8:1).

After being arrested, Stephen was falsely charged with speaking blasphemous words against God, Moses, and the temple, claiming that Jesus would destroy the temple and change the law of Moses (6:11–14). When the high priest asked Stephen, "Are these things so" (verse 1), Stephen began the longest and one of the most important speeches in the Acts of the Apostles. Through Stephen's words, the author provides the reader with an interpretation of the entire two-volume work (the gospel of Luke and the Acts of the Apostles). Covering a huge amount of the biblical story with great compression, Stephen recounts the history of salvation, beginning with Abraham and continuing through Moses, David, Solomon, and the construction of the temple. The purpose of this survey is to demonstrate that this saving history is continued in Jesus and the apostles.

The subject of the speech is clearly God. He is called "the God of glory" (verse 2). This divine title suggests the manifestation of God's presence on earth, which came to be known as the "Shekinah." This glory of God was associated primarily with the tent of God's dwelling in the wilderness and then with the temple in Jerusalem. But Stephen declares that God needs neither tent nor temple, for God manifested himself to Abraham while he was still living in Mesopotamia and was present with him throughout all his wanderings.

The first part of Stephen's speech is about what God has done in Abraham. God is the actor: God "appeared to Abraham"; God spoke to him (verses 3, 6); God showed Abraham the land; God had Abraham move to Canaan (verse 4); God promised (verse 5); God judged (verse 7); and God gave Abraham the covenant (verse 8). Stephen's emphasis is on what God has done in the past and promised for the future. Those promises of God are fulfilled in surprising ways throughout Israel's history, namely through the exodus from slavery and entry into the promised land (verses 6–7). But Stephen's primary point is that what God began in Abraham continues into the history of Jesus and his church. The promises to Abraham are being fulfilled in the messianic mission of Jesus Christ.

At the time of Luke's writing, the many factions within Judaism were competing over who was the legitimate successor to the ancient history of Israel. With the temple destroyed by the Romans (A.D. 70), the debate within the family of Judaism is over who will continue the family line, who can lay claim to authentic family membership. Stephen is in a grueling life-and-death struggle with his fellow Jews over who is the real heir of the family inheritance. Stephen argues that the people of God no longer depend on the temple in Jerusalem, nor are they ruled by the high priest and his council. Rather they are those who inherit the promises made to Abraham through participating in their fulfillment in the good news of Jesus Christ. In response to Stephen's long and pivotal speech, his antagonists dragged him outside the city gates and stoned him to death for blasphemy.

Reflection and discussion

- What is the main point of Stephen's speech? In what way is it a turning point in Luke's narrative history of the early church?

- How do the stories of Abraham convince me that God's presence cannot be confined to a particular place? Where do I most clearly experience the manifestation of God?

- In what way are the promises made to Abraham fulfilled in Jesus? In what way are they fulfilled in my life? How do I know that God is faithful?

Prayer

Risen Lord, in you all the nations of the earth are blessed and all people can respond to the good news of your saving death and resurrection. Bless me with strong faith so that I might be a witness for you.

LESSON 30  SESSION 6

From one person, and this one as good as dead, descendants were born, "as many as the stars of heaven and as the innumerable grains of sand by the seashore."

HEBREWS 11:12

The Example of Abraham's Faith

HEBREWS 11:8–19 [8]*By faith Abraham obeyed when he was called to set out for a place that he was to receive as an inheritance; and he set out, not knowing where he was going.* [9]*By faith he stayed for a time in the land he had been promised, as in a foreign land, living in tents, as did Isaac and Jacob, who were heirs with him of the same promise.* [10]*For he looked forward to the city that has foundations, whose architect and builder is God.* [11]*By faith he received power of procreation, even though he was too old—and Sarah herself was barren—because he considered him faithful who had promised.* [12]*Therefore from one person, and this one as good as dead, descendants were born, "as many as the stars of heaven and as the innumerable grains of sand by the seashore."*

[13]*All of these died in faith without having received the promises, but from a distance they saw and greeted them. They confessed that they were strangers and foreigners on the earth,* [14]*for people who speak in this way make it clear that they are seeking a homeland.* [15]*If they had been thinking of the land that they had left behind, they would have had opportunity to return.* [16]*But as it is, they desire a better country, that is, a heavenly one. Therefore God is not ashamed to be called their God; indeed, he has prepared a city for them.*

[17]By faith Abraham, when put to the test, offered up Isaac. He who had received the promises was ready to offer up his only son, [18]of whom he had been told, "It is through Isaac that descendants shall be named for you." [19]He considered the fact that God is able even to raise someone from the dead—and figuratively speaking, he did receive him back.

Above all his many qualities, Abraham is best known for his faith. According to Genesis, "Abram believed the Lord, and the Lord reckoned it to him as righteousness" (Gen 15:6). Paul described Abraham as "the ancestor of all who believe" (Rom 4:11). "Those who believe are blessed with Abraham who believed" (Gal 3:9). In the Letter to the Hebrews, the writer holds up the life of Abraham as a model of faith, highlighting three major chapters in his life.

First of all, Abraham was sent by God on a journey of faith. Abraham obeyed and departed, not knowing where he was going, trusting only that God would give him the land as an inheritance (verse 8). He left the known and familiar and entrusted his future to God. Reaching the promised land, he continued to journey in tents, like a stranger in a foreign land (verse 9). A man of faith, Abraham was utterly dependent on God and motivated only by God's promises.

The second illustration of Abraham's faith was his trusting belief in God's promises of descendants. Abraham was promised what was humanly impossible. Though he was most likely impotent and Sarah was barren, God promised Abraham that he would have descendants in abundance (verses 11–12). Abraham and Sarah received the power of procreation because they trusted in the faithfulness and trustworthiness of God.

The last example of Abraham's faith was the testing involved in the offering of Isaac. Abraham's faith in God was so strong that "he considered the fact that God is able even to raise someone from the dead" (verses 17–19). God's act of saving Isaac from death was as though God had raised him from the dead. Yet, the allusion goes beyond Isaac to the anticipation of Christ. Like Abraham, God willingly sacrificed his only Son, whom he raised from the dead through the resurrection. Belief in the power of God to raise the dead to life is the greatest faith.

The chapters of Abraham's life demonstrate the faith defined by the author of Hebrews: "Faith is the assurance of things hoped for, the conviction of things not seen" (11:1). Abraham was the pilgrim traveler—journeying toward the unseen and the unknown, acting on the basis of God's promises alone. The things hoped for guided his life, though he died without having received the promises (verse 13). He spent his life reaching for what he only glimpsed in the distance.

The promises and blessings experienced by Abraham and Sarah, as wonderful as they were, were only a shadow of the transcendent reality still to come. Like all of us, they knew that their true "homeland" was not to be found in their earthly life (verse 14). The promised land was not only a tract of real estate on the eastern shore of the Mediterranean. Abraham looked forward to "a better country" (verse 16), to "the city that has foundations," a stable and lasting city "whose architect and builder is God" (verse 10).

The faith of Abraham and Sarah was not a passive waiting; it was a lively obedience and active pilgrimage motivated by God's trustworthiness. As James wrote in his letter, Abraham's "faith was brought to completion by his works" (James 2:21–24). God's promises, the things hoped for, though not yet seen, are a powerful motivator for people of faith. Like Abraham and Sarah, we live our lives as traveling pilgrims, not always knowing where we are going, but led by God's promises. The journey is never confined to one generation; it is in opposition to the demands of our culture that wants everything now, and it is always challenging and risky. Abraham and Sarah have gone ahead of us to show us the way. As their children from among all the nations, may we be blessed through them.

For reflection

- How would I define faith in terms of my own life? In what ways are Abraham and Sarah models of faith for me?

- What obstacles did Abraham have to overcome in each of the three episodes that defined his faith?

- What three episodes of my life have best demonstrated the challenges of faith?

- How would the world be different if all the descendants of Abraham realized that they are “strangers and foreigners on the earth” (verse 13) seeking a common “homeland” (verse 14)?

Prayer

God of our ancestors, you have called us to be traveling pilgrims on the earth and have assured us that you are faithful to your promises. May we join with all the sons and daughters of Abraham as we journey together toward our final homeland with you.

SUGGESTIONS FOR FACILITATORS, GROUP SESSION 6

1. Welcome group members and make any final announcements or requests.

2. You may want to pray this prayer as a group:
   God of our fathers and mothers, you have proven your faithfulness to our ancient covenant by sending your Son as Israel's Messiah. In him the numbers of Abraham's children grow beyond counting, like the stars of the sky, and all the nations of the earth are blessed. Let your word penetrate our hearts and bless us with faith like that of Abraham and Sarah. May we give witness to your faithfulness and serve you all our days.

3. Ask one of the following questions:
   - How has this study of Abraham and Sarah enriched your life?
   - In what way has this study challenged you the most?

4. Discuss lessons 25 through 30. Choose one or more of the questions for reflection and discussion from each lesson to discuss as a group.

5. Ask the group if they would like to study another title in the *Threshold Bible Study* series. Discuss the topic and dates, and make a decision among those interested. Ask the group members to suggest people they would like to invite to participate in the next study series.

6. Ask the group to discuss the insights that stand out most from this study over the past six weeks.

7. Conclude by praying aloud the following prayer or another of your own choosing:
   Holy Spirit of the living God, you inspired the writers of the Scriptures and you have guided our study during these weeks. Continue to deepen our love for the word of God in the holy Scriptures and draw us more deeply into the heart of Jesus. We thank you for the confident hope you have placed within us and the gifts which build up the church. Through this study, lead us to worship and witness more fully and fervently, and bless us now and always with the fire of your love.